MERRY
CHRISTMAS
SONGBOOK

MERRY CHRISTMAS SONGBOOK

Editor: William L. Simon
Music arranged and edited by Dan Fox
Editorial Associates: Mary Kelleher, Elizabeth Mead, Natalie Moreda
Art and Design: Karen Mastropietro
Annotated by Dorothy Horstman and the Editors
Director, Rights & Permissions: Lisa Garrett Smith
Associate, Rights & Permissions: Arlene Pasciolla

The Reader's Digest Association, Inc.
Pleasantville, New York • Montreal

A Reader's Digest Book

Copyright © 2007 The Reader's Digest Association, Inc.
Copyright © 2007 The Reader's Digest Association (Canada) Ltd.

Editions of the *Merry Christmas Songbook* without a CD have been previously published:
    ISBN 0-7621-0463-5
    ISBN 0-89577-105-5

ISBN 978-0-7621-0868-8

We are committed to both the quality of our products and the service we provide to our customers.
We value your comments, so please feel free to contact us:
    The Reader's Digest Association, Inc.
    Adult Trade Publishing
    Reader's Digest Road
    Pleasantville, NY 10570-7000

For more Reader's Digest products and information, visit our website:
    www.rd.com (in the United States)
    www.readersdigest.ca (in Canada)

This book is printed on environmentally friendly paper,
certified by FSC (Forest Stewardship Council).

Printed in China

1 3 5 7 9 10 8 6 4 2

Index to Sections

Index to Songs

INTRODUCTION

Christmas is a special time—a time of rejoicing, of solemn thanksgiving, of gift-giving, of pleasures both modern and traditional, of feasting and of being together with family and friends.

And Christmas is a time of special music. What better way to celebrate the birthday of Jesus than to join together and raise our voices in the special songs of Christmas—or to tune our musical instruments and play the timeless melodies that have come to us over the years?

That's what *The Reader's Digest Merry Christmas Songbook* is all about, sharing with loved ones and fellow worshipers the joy of this most precious time of the year. Here, within the covers of this book, is a collection of 108 favorite songs and instrumentals that, year after year, will help to make the holiday season even more memorable.

Take a minute now to thumb through the book, and you'll find most of your familiar favorites, as well as many songs you've always wanted to learn to play and sing. There are songs of every kind, specially selected to touch the heart of every member of the family—from your favorite carols to classic instrumentals, from novelties that will make the children laugh to traditional favorites that will bring a tear to the eyes of their elders.

Santa Claus is here, of course, as well as Rudolph the Red-Nosed Reindeer, Frosty the Snow Man, King Wenceslas, the Three Kings, the little drummer boy and, most important, the Christ Child.

This is a Christmas songbook that will remain open long after the magic day has passed, for it also contains many popular winter songs, and even some songs to welcome in the New Year. There are popular songs, modern carols that are well on their way to becoming classics, folk songs and spirituals, plus an international selection of favorites, several in the original language as well as in English.

In addition to the outstanding selection of Christmas songs, this volume offers a number of other features. As with all of our Reader's Digest music books, we have used the convenient spiral binding that enables the pages to lie flat when the book is open. We have taken special pains to make most of the songs self-contained on one page or on facing pages to keep page-turning to a minimum. Another feature that gives the *Merry Christmas Songbook* its unique readability: Wherever a song has more than two stanzas, a faint tint runs through each alternate line, making it easy to keep your eyes on the proper place when singing. And on special tinted pages at the beginning of each section, you will find insightful annotations for the songs in that section.

Also, we have taken the usual care with the arrangements to make them easy to play and sing, yet truly professional-sounding and musically interesting. For this, we have arranger and composer Dan Fox to thank. Dan is familiar to buyers of The Reader's Digest music books for his arrangements for those books, as well as for more than 200 other publications. He is a "serious" composer, too, and has scored a symphony, an opera, a cantata and many chamber works. You'll be able to detect his skillful hand throughout.

Now, just a few words on how to use this book to gain the greatest enjoyment. Except for the strictly instrumental numbers, every song features a vocal melody line with piano or organ accompaniment. The melody line is easy to recognize because the stems of the notes go up, while on the harmony notes, the stems go down. This same line can be followed by any solo C-melody instrument, including violin, flute, recorder, oboe, accordion and harmonica.

For guitarists, three systems of notation are provided: chord names, simple diagrams and, of course, the melody line. Dan Fox himself is a master guitarist, which explains the smooth progressions and expert voicings of these arrangements.

Players of electronic organs (not the limited "by-the-numbers" chord models) will find appropriate pedal notations at the bottom of the bass clef. *They're the smaller notes*, with the stems turned downward. These notes are *only* for organ pedals; don't try to play them on the piano.

Accordionists should play the right hand as written and use the chord symbols as a guide for the left-hand buttons. And bass players, whether string or brass, can play the root note of each chord symbol, except where another note is specified, as "G/D bass."

As you can see, this single musical volume can serve an entire instrumental ensemble, a soloist or an old-fashioned sing-along.

Whatever your taste in music, whatever your proficiency with a musical instrument, whether you like to sing alone or sing along, you will find much in this volume that is rewarding. We hope it gives you as much joy at this holiday season—and for many years to come—as it gave us in putting it together. Merry Christmas!

— THE EDITORS

Section One
Our Best-Loved Carols

Angels We Have Heard on High (*Traditional*)

Many years ago, shepherds tending their flocks in the wintry hills of southern France had a custom of calling to one another on Christmas Eve, each from his own peak, singing "Gloria in excelsis Deo, gloria in excelsis Deo," just as the angels might have first announced the birth of Christ. The traditional tune the shepherds used, probably from a late medieval Latin chorale, is the refrain of "Angels We Have Heard on High." The music for the verse—probably 18th century—comes from a different source (a popular tune of the time), as does the text itself, a translation of the old French carol "Les Anges dans nos Campagnes." They were first published together in a carol collection dated 1855.

Away in a Manger (*Traditional*)

Martin Luther, the German religious reformer, wrote a number of beautiful and stirring hymns and hymn texts, but this sweet lullaby is not among them–although it has been widely credited to him. For reasons of his own, one James R. Murray published this verse in 1887 in a collection called Dainty Songs for Lads and Lasses, *labeling it "Luther's Cradle Hymn, composed by Martin Luther for his children, and still sung by German mothers to their little ones," and then adding his own initials, J.R.M., to confuse the matter further. The poem, however, was not Luther's or Murray's, but rather was "borrowed" from a children's Sunday school book published a couple of years earlier in Philadelphia. The origin of the tune used here is also uncertain, although it is possible that Murray was its composer. The words are also often sung to the melody used for the Scottish poem "Flow Gently, Sweet Afton."*

Deck the Halls (*Old Welsh Air*)

Although most of us now live in rooms rather than vast, vaulted halls, we still deck them out at Christmastime–with holly, wreaths, flowers, colors, anything our imaginations can conjure up. The old traditions suggested by this song would seem to indicate that it is of ancient English vintage. But, although the origins of the melody are shrouded in antiquity, with indications that it originated in Wales, the familiar words, whose origins are also obscure, are believed to be American. And if you wonder why American lyrics would make such a point of celebrating old English customs, the answer is that they were produced in the United States in the 19th century when Washington Irving was glorifying English customs and Charles Dickens' A Christmas Carol was at the height of its first popularity.

The First Noël (*Traditional*)

The Christmas song telling the story of "The First Noël" ("Noël" is the French word for Christmas and stems from the Latin natalis, *meaning "birthday") is thought to date from as early as the 13th or 14th century, when the Miracle Plays, dramatizations of favorite Bible stories for special holidays, were growing popular. The tune, which may be English or French, is undoubtedly very old. It was first published with words by William Sandys in his 1833 edition of* Christmas Carols, Ancient and Modern.

God Rest Ye Merry, Gentlemen (*Traditional*) *Page 14*

"God Rest Ye Merry, Gentlemen" is one of the carols that was sung by the waits, those municipal watchmen in old England who, like the town criers, were licensed to perform certain duties, such as singing seasonal songs, including those of Christmas, to the proper people. It was first published in 1827 as "an ancient version, sung in the streets of London." Charles Dickens used it in A Christmas Carol: Ebenezer Scrooge, the rich but miserly curmudgeon, hears it sung jauntily in the street and threatens to hit the singer with a ruler if he does not cease immediately. Fortunately, Scrooge is about to be vouchsafed the true meaning of Christmas, and to be made merry—and generous—himself.

Good King Wenceslas (*Words by John Mason Neale; Music Traditional*) *Page 38*

Yes, Virginia, there was indeed a noble Wenceslas. He was not a king, however, but the Duke of Bohemia. He was a good and honest and strongly principled man, as the song about him indicates—too good, perhaps, because in 929 he was murdered by his envious and wicked younger brother. In 1853, John Mason Neale, an English divine, selected the martyr Wenceslas as the subject for a children's song to exemplify generosity. It quickly became a Christmas favorite, even though its words clearly indicate that Wenceslas "look'd out" on St. Stephen's Day, the day after Christmas. For a tune, Neale picked a spring carol, originally sung with the Latin text "Tempus adest floridum," or "Spring has unwrapped her flowers," which was first published in 1582 in a collection of Swedish church and school songs.

Hark! the Herald Angels Sing *Page 16*
(*Words by Charles Wesley; Music by Felix Mendelssohn*)

Felix Mendelssohn composed the energetic tune to which we now sing "Hark! the Herald Angels Sing" in 1840 as part of a cantata commemorating printer Johann Gutenberg. Fifteen years later an English musician, W. H. Cummings, applied Mendelssohn's musical phrases to a hymn written in 1739 by Charles Wesley. ("Hark, how all the welkin [heaven] rings" was how Wesley wrote the line; fortunately, a colleague substituted the opening line we know and sing today.) The devout Wesley, the Poet Laureate of Methodism, composed about 6,500 hymns in the course of his life. He and his equally devout brother John, who founded Methodism in England, might have been dismayed by the sprightly character of the music, but their text would have pleased Mendelssohn, who always felt that his tune deserved a "merry subject."

Here We Come A-Caroling (The Wassail Song) (*Traditional*) *Page 40*

"Here We Come A-Caroling" is an old English wassail song, or a song to which good health, which is what "wassail" means. In days of yore, the Christmas spirit often made the rich a little more generous than usual, and bands of beggars and orphans used to dance their way through the snowy streets of England, offering to sing good cheer and to tell good fortune if the householder would give them a drink from his wassail bowl, or a penny, or a pork pie or, better yet, let them stand for a few minutes beside the warmth of his hearth. The wassail bowl itself was a hearty combination of hot ale or beer and spices and mead, just alcoholic enough to warm the tingling toes and fingers of the singers.

It Came Upon the Midnight Clear *Page 24*
(*Words by Edmund Hamilton Sears; Music by Richard Storrs Willis*)

Oliver Wendell Holmes once declared this hymn by Edmund Hamilton Sears to be "one of the finest and most beautiful ever written." Sears, a retiring young Unitarian minister in Massachusetts, was dismayed by such public praise, saying he preferred to lead a quiet life in some half-forgotten parish. Fame dogged him, however, as well it might when "It Came Upon the Midnight Clear" was one of his early efforts. The poem was first published in 1849 in a church magazine and was adapted the following year to a tune composed by Richard Storrs Willis. Willis, by that time an eminent editor and critic for the New York Tribune, had studied music in Europe as a young man, with, among others, Felix Mendelssohn, who so much admired Willis's work that he rearranged some of it for orchestra.

Section One: Our Best-Loved Carols

Joy to the World (*Words by Isaac Watts; Music by Lowell Mason*)   *Page 26*

Though the triumphant words "Joy to the world" exemplify the Christmas feeling, this familiar text is actually a translation based on five verses from Psalm 98 in the Old Testament. Isaac Watts, the English hymnist and cleric, published his Psalms of David, which contains these verses, in 1719. More than a century later, in 1839, American composer and music educator Lowell Mason decided to set them to music, modestly including the phrase "From George Frederick Handel," apparently to honor his idol, the composer of Messiah and many other master-pieces. For nearly 100 years, the world accepted this ascription, until musicologists pointed out that not a single phrase in the music can be said to have come straight from any work of Handel's.

O Christmas Tree (O Tannenbaum) (*Traditional*)   *Page 22*

Centuries ago, a lovely legend arose that on the night Jesus was born all the trees in the forests everywhere–in Africa where the night was warm, in Iceland where the night was frosty–bloomed and bore their most delicate fruit. Another legend exists, too, that Martin Luther, striding through the woods late one Christmas Eve, noticed how exquisitely pure the starlight seemed when glimpsed through the trees, so he took home an evergreen as a remembrance of that Christmas night and decorated it with candles to simulate the stars. Whatever the true story of the first Christmas tree, the custom of decorating trees at Christmas arose in Germany. Today there is no more universal holiday deco-ration. The most popular carol about the Christmas tree is this one from Germany, "O Christmas Tree," also known as "O Tannenbaum."

O Come, All Ye Faithful (Adeste Fideles)   *Page 30*
(*English words by Frederick Oakeley;*
Latin words attributed to John Francis Wade; Music by John Reading)

John Francis Wade was an 18th-century British exile who moved to a Roman Catholic community in France, where he eked out an income by copying and selling music, and by giving music lessons to children. Perhaps he himself wrote the Latin stanzas, beginning "Adeste fideles," which have made his name known; perhaps they were a text he was called upon to translate. In any case, he combined the text with a bit of music, probably by another Englishman, John Reading, and published the resulting hymn around 1751. More than a century later, the English version, "O Come, All Ye Faithful," was turned out by Frederick Oakeley, a British clergyman who felt that if congregations had good literary texts to sing, they would sing well. This hymn proved his point.

O Little Town of Bethlehem   *Page 18*
(*Words by Phillips Brooks; Music by Lewis H. Redner*)

Phillips Brooks, one of 19th-century America's best-loved preachers, was ministering to a Philadelphia church when he wrote his now-famous verses at Christmastime in 1868. He had journeyed to the Holy Land three years earlier, and the memory was, he said, "still singing in my soul." His organist, Lewis Redner, who was professionally a high-ly successful real-estate broker and on Sundays a leader in the Sunday school, set Brooks' words to music for the church's children's choir, and "O Little Town of Bethlehem" was subsequently taken up by the rest of the world.

Silent Night   *Page 13*
(*English words adapted from the original German of Joseph Mohr;*
Music by Franz Gruber)

On the afternoon of Christmas Eve in 1818, in a tiny village high in the Austrian Alps, Joseph Mohr, the local Catholic priest, wrote some appropriate stanzas for the season. The church pipe organ had given out and could not be repaired in time for that evening, so the church organist, Franz Gruber, wrote a simple tune, setting the words for a tenor, a bass and two guitars. That very evening, at the midnight service, "Silent Night" was heard for the first time. The song soon made its way beyond the town of Oberdorf, but anonymously, without mention of composer or poet. Until the 1850s, neither Gruber nor Mohr, living in their remote village, knew that their song was rapidly becoming the most beloved piece of Christmas music ever written—nor did the world know of Gruber and Mohr.

The Twelve Days of Christmas (*Traditional*) *Page 32*

In the Middle Ages, religious holidays were practically the only holidays, so lord and peasant alike tried to extend such happy times as long as possible. Christmas became not one day of celebration but 12, extending from Christmas Day to the Epiphany, when the Wise Men arrived with their gifts (thereby initiating the custom of giving presents at Christmas). In the castles of the wealthy, a gift on each of the 12 days was not unusual. Hence the appeal of "The Twelve Days of Christmas," since even those who couldn't afford to give the gifts could at least sing about them. The carol is very old, dating probably from the 16th century, when such sprightly counting songs were very much in fashion.

We Three Kings of Orient Are (*Words and Music by John Henry Hopkins*) *Page 20*

In 1857, John Henry Hopkins, Jr., assembled an elaborate Christmas pageant, for which he wrote both words and music, for the General Theological Seminary in New York City, where he was an instructor in church music. One of the selections dealt with the Wise Men who came from the East, and for this part of the pageant, Hopkins created one of America's most beloved carols. The three kings, Melchior, Caspar and Balthazar, brought: gold, traditionally the metal of royalty; frankincense, an aromatic bark whose smoke was thought to reach the gates of heaven; and myrrh, an unguent used in the preparation of bodies for burial. The gifts thus signified Jesus' kingship, His oneness with God, and His eventual death on the cross.

We Wish You a Merry Christmas (*Traditional*) *Page 42*

In the days of Merrie Olde England, a good part of life went on to the sound of music. Rich merchants hired bands to accompany them on strolls; peddlers enhanced their sales pitches with song; and a municipal chorus of singers, called waits, were licensed to sing out the hours of day or night, to greet visiting dignitaries, and to enliven weddings of the rich and near-rich. Waits were especially busy at Christmastime, serenading on frosty nights, telling the Nativity story in song, and generally making the festivities of that favorite holiday even merrier. In return, they might receive coins, or a bit of fig pudding, spiced ale or roasted pig. Many of the oldest carols are waits' carols, including "We Wish You a Merry Christmas."

Silent Night

English words adapted from the original German of Joseph Mohr; Music by Franz Gruber

1. Si - lent night, ho - ly night, All is calm, all is bright.
2. Si - lent night, ho - ly night, Shep-herds quake at the sight.
3. Si - lent night, ho - ly night, Son of God, love's pure light;

(1) Round yon Vir - gin Moth-er and Child, Ho - ly In-fant so ten-der and mild,
(2) Glo - ries stream from heav-en a - far, Heav'n-ly hosts sing Al - le - lu - ia;
(3) Ra - diant beams from Thy ho - ly face, With the dawn of re-deem-ing grace,

(1) Sleep in heav-en-ly peace; Sleep in heav-en-ly peace.
(2) Christ the Sav - ior is born; Christ the Sav - ior is born.
(3) Je - sus, Lord, at Thy birth; Je - sus, Lord, at Thy birth.

13

God Rest Ye Merry, Gentlemen

Traditional

Moderately, in two (♩=1 beat)

mf

1. God

Em

(1) rest ye mer - ry, gen - tle - men; let noth - ing you dis - may. Re-
(2) Beth - le - hem, in Is - ra - el, this bless - ed Babe was born, And
(3) God our heav'n - ly Fa - ther, a bless - ed an - gel came; And

(R.H.)

(1) mem - ber, Christ our Sav - ior was born on Christ - mas Day To
(2) laid with - in a man - ger up - on this bless - ed morn; The
(3) un - to cer - tain shep - herds brought tid - ings of the same; How

Words by Charles Wesley
Music by Felix Mendelssohn

Hark! the Herald Angels Sing

1. Hark! the her - ald an - gels sing,___ "Glo - ry to the
2. Christ by high - est heav'n a - dored;___ Christ the ev - er -
3. Hail the heav'n - born Prince of Peace!___ Hail the Son of

(1) new - born King! Peace on earth and mer - cy mild,___
(2) last - ing Lord! Late in time be - hold Him come,___
(3) Righ - teous - ness! Light and life to all He brings,___

O Little Town of Bethlehem

Words by Phillips Brooks; Music by Lewis H. Redner

DECK THE HALLS

Old Welsh Air

Deck the halls with boughs of hol - ly,
Fa la la la la la la la la.
See the blaz - ing Yule be - fore us,
Fa la la la la la la la la.

'Tis the sea - son to be jol - ly,
Fa la la la la la la la la.
Strike the harp and join the cho - rus,
Fa la la la la la la la la.

Don we now our gay ap - par - el,
Fa__ la, fa__ la la la la.
Fol - low me in mer - ry mea - sure,
Fa__ la, fa__ la la la la.

Troll the an - cient Yule - tide car - ol,
Fa la la la la la la la la.
While I tell of Yule - tide trea - sure,
Fa la la la la la la la la.

19

We Three Kings of Orient Are

Words and Music by John Henry Hopkins

1. We three kings of O - ri - ent are,
2. Born a King on Beth - le - hem's plain,
3. Frank - in - cense to of - fer have I,
4. Myrrh is mine, its bit - ter per - fume
5. Glo - rious now be - hold Him a - rise,

(1) Bear - ing gifts we tra - verse a - far, Field and foun - tain,
(2) Gold I bring to crown Him a - gain, King for - ev - er,
(3) In - cense owns a De - i - ty nigh. Pray'r and prais - ing,
(4) Breathes of life of gath - er - ing gloom; Sor - row - ing, sigh - ing,
(5) King and God and Sac - ri - fice. Al - le - lu - ia,

(1) moor and moun - tain, Fol - low - ing yon - der star.
(2) ceas - ing nev - er, O - ver us all to reign.
(3) all men rais - ing, Wor - ship Him, God most high.
(4) bleed - ing, dy - ing, Sealed in the stone - cold tomb.
(5) Al - le - lu - ia, Earth to heav'n re - plies.

O____

Chorus

Star of won - der, Star of night,

Star with roy - al beau - ty bright,

West - ward lead - ing, still pro - ceed - ing,

D. C. for additional words

Guide us to Thy per - fect light.

O Christmas Tree
O Tannenbaum

Traditional

Moderately

Christ-mas tree, O Christ-mas tree, thy leaves are so un-chang-ing. O
Christ-mas tree, O Christ-mas tree, you fill all hearts with gai-ety. O
Tan - nen-baum, O Tan - nen-baum, wie treu sind dei - ne Blät - ter.

Christ-mas tree, O Christ-mas tree, thy leaves are so un-chang-ing. Not
Christ-mas tree, O Christ-mas tree, you fill all hearts with gai-ety. On
(Instrumental to - - - - - - - - - - - - - - - - - -) Du

23

It Came Upon the Midnight Clear

Words by Edmund Hamilton Sears
Music by Richard Storrs Willis

Moderately

(1) came up-on__ the mid-night clear That glo-rious song__ of
(2) through the clo-ven skies they come With peace-ful wings__ un-
(3) lo! the days__ are has-t'ning on, By proph-ets seen__ of

(1) old,__ From an-gels bend-ing near the earth To touch their harps__ of
(2) furl'd;__ And still their heav'n-ly mu-sic floats O'er all the wea-ry
(3) old,__ When with the ev-er-cir-cling years Shall come the time__ fore-

Joy to the World

Words by Isaac Watts; Music by Lowell Mason

1. Joy to the world! the Lord has (1) come: Let earth re - ceive her King. Let
2. Joy to the world! the Sav - ior (2) reigns: Let men their songs em - ploy, While
3. He rules the world with truth and (3) grace, And makes the na - tions prove The

The First Noël

Traditional

Moderately

(1) 1. The first Noël, the an-gel did say,
(2) 2. They look-ed up and saw a star,
(3) 3. This star drew nigh to the north-

(1) say, Was to cer-tain poor shep-herds in
(2) star, Shin-ing in the East be it
(3) west; O'er Beth-le-hem it

(1) fields as they lay; In fields where
(2) yond them far; And to the
(3) took its rest, And there it

(1) they lay keep - ing their sheep, On a
(2) earth it gave great light, And
(3) did both stop and stay, Right

(1) cold win - ter's night that was so deep.)
(2) so it con - tin - ued day and night.}
(3) o'er the place where Je - sus lay.

Chorus

No - ël, No - ël, No - ël, No - ël,

Born is the King of Is - ra - el.

O Come, All Ye Faithful

Adeste Fideles

English words by Frederick Oakeley; Latin words attributed to John Francis Wade; Music by John Reading

Broadly

O come, all ye faith - ful, Joy - ful and tri - um - phant, O come ye, O come____ ye to Beth - le-hem. Come and be - hold Him,

A - des - te fi - de - les, Lae - ti tri - um - phan - tes, Ve - ni - te, ve - ni - te in Beth - le-hem. Na - tum vi - de - te,

Chorus

born the King of an - gels. O come, let us a -
Re - gem an - ge - lo - rum. Ve - ni - te a - do -

dore Him; O come, let us a - dore Him; O
re - mus; Ve - ni - te a - do - re - mus; Ve -

come, let us a - dore Him,____ Christ,____ the Lord.
ni - te a - do - re - mus,____ Do - mi - num.

2. Sing, choirs of angels,
   Sing in exultation;
   Sing all ye citizens of heav'n above:
   Glory to God in the Highest.
   Chorus

3. Yea, Lord, we greet Thee,
   Born this happy morning;
   Jesus, to Thee be glory giv'n;
   Word of the Father, now in flesh appearing.
   Chorus

The Twelve Days of Christmas

Traditional

Away in a Manger

Traditional

Tenderly

1. A - way in a man - ger, no crib for a bed, The lit - tle Lord
2. The cat - tle are low - ing, the poor Ba - by wakes, But lit - tle Lord
3. Be near me, Lord Je - sus, I ask Thee to stay Close by me for-

(1) Je - sus laid down His sweet head. The stars in the sky_____ looked
(2) Je - sus no cry - ing He makes. I love Thee, Lord Je - sus, look
(3) ev - er and love me I pray. Bless all the dear chil - dren in

(1) down where He lay, The lit - tle Lord Je - sus a - sleep on the hay.
(2) down from the sky, And stay by my cra - dle till morn - ing is nigh.
(3) Thy ten - der care, And take us to heav-en to live with Thee there.

Angels We Have Heard on High

Traditional

Joyously

1. An - gels we have heard on high Sweet - ly sing - ing o'er the plains,
2. Shep - herds, why this ju - bi - lee? Why your joy - ous strains pro - long?
3. Come to Beth - le - hem and see Him whose birth the an - gels sing.

(1) And the moun - tains in re - ply Ech - o - ing their joy - ous strains.
(2) What the glad - some tid - ings be Which in - spire your heav'n - ly song?
(3) Come a - dore on bend - ed knee Christ the Lord, the new - born King.

Good King Wenceslas

Words by John Mason Neale; Music Traditional

HERE WE COME A-CAROLING
THE WASSAIL SONG

Traditional

With spirit

1 Here we come a-car-ol-ing a-mong the leaves so green;
(2) are not dai-ly beg-gars that beg from door to door, But
(3) bless the mas-ter of this house, like-wise the mis-tress too, And

(1) Here we come a-wan-d'ring so fair____ to be seen.
(2) we are neigh-bors' chil-dren whom you have seen be-fore.
(3) all the lit-tle chil-dren that round the ta-ble go.

We Wish You a Merry Christmas

Traditional

Brightly, with spirit

Chorus

(1) wish you a Mer-ry Christ-mas; We wish you a Mer-ry Christ-mas; We
(2) bring us a fig-gy pud-ding; Oh, bring us a fig-gy pud-ding; Oh,
(3) won't go un-til we've got some; We won't go un-til we've got some; We

(1) wish you a Mer-ry Christ-mas and a Hap-py New Year.
(2) bring us a fig-gy pud-ding and a cup of good cheer. Good
(3) won't go un-til we've got some, so bring some out here.

tid - ings to you wher - ev - er you are; Good

tid - ings for Christ-mas and a Hap - py New Year. 2. Oh,*(repeat)*
3. We *(repeat)*
4. We *(continue)*

wish you a Mer-ry Christ-mas; We wish you a Mer-ry Christ-mas; We

wish you a Mer-ry Christ-mas and a Hap - py New Year.

Section Two
Popular Christmas Hits

Blue Christmas *(Words and Music by Billy Hayes and Jay Johnson)*   Page 60

Most Christmas songs are filled with warmth, hope and good cheer in celebration of our most beloved holiday. But there's another side to Christmas, too, with special appeal to the country and western music audience. The theme of lost and unrequited love is familiar to all country fans, and here it is given a poignant twist by songwriters Billy Hayes and Jay Johnson. "Blue Christmas" was written in 1948, and country singer Ernest Tubb made it a hit that same year. Both Elvis Presley and Hugo Winterhalter had popular versions of the song, but it remains steadfastly a country classic.

C-H-R-I-S-T-M-A-S *(Words by Jenny Lou Carson; Music by Eddy Arnold)*   Page 76

Country singer Eddy Arnold's contribution to Christmas, which he wrote in 1949 with Jenny Lou Carson, is a reminder of the day's true meaning. "C-H-R-I-S-T-M-A-S" makes an acronym of the true symbols of Christmas: C for the Christ Child; H for the herald angels; R for the Redeemer; I for Israel, where Christ was born; S for the star that guided T, the three Wise Men; M for the manger where Jesus lay; A for all Christ means to each of us; and S for the shepherds, the first to enter the stable in worship. Both Eddy Arnold and Jim Reeves made classic recordings of this little song with its simple melody.

Christmas for Cowboys *(Words and Music by Steve Weisberg)*   Page 68

Steve Weisberg was born and raised in Dallas, but he makes no claim to being a cowboy (though he does think that cowboy boots are the only appropriate footwear). In 1975, Weisberg, playing lead guitar, was recording a Christmas album in Los Angeles with singer John Denver. Though Denver usually writes and records his own material, the album was one song short, and Weisberg got his chance. Using a melody that he had had in mind for a while, he stayed up all night and came up with "Christmas for Cowboys," which soon became a part of Denver's Rocky Mountain Christmas *album.*

Christmas in Killarney   Page 54
(Words and Music by John Redmond, James Cavanaugh and Frank Weldon)

Down in the southwest corner of Ireland, not far from Tralee and Killorglin and Cahirciveen, is the picturesque town of Killarney. Spring is greener there and summer is lovelier, the residents say, just because it's Killarney (rhymes with "blarney"). And in Killarney Christmas is more Christmasy, agreed the writers of this song, John Redmond, James Cavanaugh and Frank Weldon (Irishmen all). Dennis Day, the Irish tenor whose voice was compounded of the greenest shamrocks, introduced this lyrical ballad in 1951 with a recording that quickly became a best-seller.

Christmas Is *(Words by Spence Maxwell; Music by Percy Faith)*   Page 70

Percy Faith, so well known for his lush, super-symphonic arrangements of popular and semiclassical favorites, also turned his hand to songwriting. In 1966, with lyricist Spence Maxwell, he composed "Christmas Is," a gleaming compendium of some of the things that make Christmas Christmas—the sights of holly, tinsel, sparkling snow and Santa, and the sounds of bells, carols and children's laughter. What makes our holiday of holidays so special, though, is not gifts and feasting, but the feelings—the sharing, the remembering, the hoping—that make it a season of joy for all men.

The Christmas Song (Chestnuts Roasting on an Open Fire)   Page 47
(Lyric and Music by Mel Tormé and Robert Wells)

In 1946, Mel Tormé known as "The Velvet Fog," made the holiday season considerably brighter with the song he wrote (with lyrics by his friend Robert Wells) about the indoor and outdoor joys of the Yuletide season. It was "The Christmas Song," also frequently called by its first line—"Chestnuts roasting on an open fire." Jack Frost, carolers, people dressed up like Eskimos—these are part of the outdoor fun. Inside we have the smell of turkey roasting, tiny tots with their eyes glowing and the promise of Santa's visit down the chimney. Nat King Cole's 1946 recording of the song has become a perennial Christmas classic.

The Christmas Waltz *(Words by Sammy Cahn; Music by Jule Styne)* *Page 86*

The famous songwriting team of Sammy Cahn and Jule Styne ("Let It Snow! Let It Snow! Let It Snow!") was also responsible for the 1954 tune "The Christmas Waltz." Cahn told of how it came about: "Every time we would get ready to write a song together, Jule Styne would warm up at the piano by playing a tango and a Viennese-sounding waltz. One day Jule came to me and said, 'Frank Sinatra wants a Christmas song.' I said, 'How could anybody do a Christmas song after Bing Crosby did "White Christmas"?' But Jule said, 'Sammy, Frank wants a Christmas song!' So I said, 'Okay then, would you mind slowing down "Vienna"?' And that's how Jule Styne and I wrote 'The Christmas Waltz.' "

Have Yourself a Merry Little Christmas *Page 50*
(Words and Music by Hugh Martin and Ralph Blane)

There was always something of the vulnerable child about Judy Garland. Her biggest leap to fame came as a young starlet when she played little Dorothy in The Wizard of Oz *in 1939. Five years later, she had hardly grown up at all, but her eyes were just as liquid, her mouth just as prone to a quiver and her way with a song still absolutely unforgettable. That was 1944, and she was starring in* Meet Me in St. Louis, *"a love of a film," as one critic put it. In addition to "The Trolley Song" and "The Boy Next Door," the musical score by Hugh Martin and Ralph Blane offered "Have Yourself a Merry Little Christmas"—so movingly done in the Garland style that a box of tissues became almost a necessity for moviegoers.*

I'll Be Home for Christmas *Page 52*
(Words by Kim Gannon; Music by Walter Kent)

In 1943 the world was at war, and many thousands of American men and women in the service would be spending Christmas far from home. As a special gift to them and their families came this lovely, tender ballad, recorded by Bing Crosby. Just a year earlier, Bing had had a best-seller with Irving Berlin's "White Christmas," and his recording of this new song by Kim Gannon and Walter Kent also passed the million-record mark in sales. On December 17, 1965, the Crosby recording became the first "request" that was broadcast into outer space. As astronauts James Lovell and Frank Borman were hurtling back to earth aboard Gemini 7 *after their record 206 orbits, a NASA transmitter asked if there was any music they would especially like to hear. Their immediate reply? Bing's "I'll Be Home for Christmas."*

The Little Boy That Santa Claus Forgot *Page 65*
(Words and Music by Tommie Connor, Jimmy Leach and Michael Carr)

Written in 1937 by three Englishmen, "The Little Boy That Santa Claus Forgot" is in the tradition of what song scholar Sigmund Spaeth called "The Songs of Self Pity." Sentimental songs, especially those about a poor or unhappy or dying child, date back to the Victorian Era, and enjoyed a resurgence of popularity during the 1930s and into the '40s. In fact, the tradition has been kept alive in many country songs to this day. This sample was recorded by Nat King Cole, who made many Christmas songs popular hits.

The Merry Christmas Polka *Page 56*
(Words by Paul Francis Webster; Music by Sonny Burke)

Polkas first achieved popularity in the United States during the 1930s, though their appeal remained largely an ethnic one until 1948, when bandleader Frankie Yankovic, who had begun including polka versions of popular songs in his repertoire, scored a major hit with "Just Because." Even before that, though, The Andrews Sisters made the "Beer Barrel Polka" one of the most memorable songs of World War II. The '40s saw the floodgates open, and polkas and polka versions became proven sellers. Lyricist Paul Francis Webster, one of the proudest products of Tin Pan Alley, wrote many hits with a host of legendary collaborators beginning in 1928. He won three Academy Awards: for "Secret Love," "Love Is a Many-Splendored Thing" and "The Shadow of Your Smile." He teamed up with noted composer Sonny Burke to write this Christmas song, polka-style, in 1949.

Rockin' Around the Christmas Tree *(Words and Music by Johnny Marks)* *Page 84*

Johnny Marks was a man of many achievements. His Phi Beta Kappa key represents what his head could do, and such inspirational songs as "Anyone Can Move a Mountain" demonstrate what his heart could do. And his "Rudolph the Red-Nosed Reindeer" is a phenomenon on both levels — and the second most popular Christmas song ever written. "Rockin' Around the Christmas Tree" is another favorite, written by Marks in 1958, when rock 'n' roll was affecting even Christmas music. Brenda Lee's 1958 recording was a big hit. The scene is the Christmas hop, and the dancing is being done in that "new old-fashioned way."

Take Me Back to Toyland *(Words by Kal Mann; Music by Bernie Lowe)* Page 74

In the late 1950s and early '60s, Kal Mann and Bernie Lowe seemed to specialize in the exuberant rock 'n' roll songs and dances of the era. Mann discovered and managed "twister" Chubby Checker and wrote "Let's Twist Again" for him. From there, he set dance floors rocking to "The Wah-Watusi," "Hully Gully Baby" and "The Bristol Stomp." Together with Lowe he wrote "(Let Me Be Your) Teddy Bear," a hit for Elvis Presley in 1957, and "Wild One," sung by Bobby Rydell in 1960. But in 1955, the Philadelphia-born team came up with a much gentler song. Taking their cue from Victor Herbert, they composed the waltzing "Take Me Back to Toyland," a perfect tune for the Christmas season.

That's What I Want for Christmas Page 79
(Words by Irving Caesar; Music by Gerald Marks)

Written for a 1936 Shirley Temple movie, Stowaway, *"That's What I Want for Christmas" was not an integral part of the film, but was tagged on at the end. The lyrics are typical of those that Shirley Temple did so well as a child, and reading them, one can almost hear her singing the song. Irving Caesar, one of the pioneers of American popular songwriting, wrote lyrics for Broadway shows and movies with some of the greatest composers of the century, including George Gershwin, Vincent Youmans, Sigmund Romberg and his collaborator on "That's What I Want for Christmas," Gerald Marks. Marks, who also wrote for the stage and screen, is credited with a number of classics, among them "All of Me" and "Is It True What They Say About Dixie?," which he also wrote in 1936 with Irving Caesar.*

We Need a Little Christmas *(Lyrics and Music by Jerry Herman)* Page 62

*One of the jolliest of modern Christmas anthems came to us from the Broadway stage. Jerry Herman, whose scores (*Milk and Honey, Dear World, Mack and Mabel *and, of course,* Hello, Dolly!, Mame *and* La Cage aux Folles*) have earned all sorts of awards, wrote "We Need a Little Christmas" in 1966 for* Mame. *Based on Patrick Dennis's autobiographical novel (later a play and a movie)* Auntie Mame, *the musical told of the unconventional Mame Dennis (Angela Lansbury) and her nephew Patrick. Depressed and down-on-their-luck, Mame and Patrick, joined by their servants Agnes Gooch and Ito the butler, sing that, even though it's too early in the year, they need the holly, the candles, the carols, the laughter, the singing—the* spirit *that only Christmas can bring.*

Welcome Christmas (From "How the Grinch Stole Christmas") Page 72
(Music by Albert Hague; lyrics by Dr. Seuss)

For many hundreds of years, "Welcome Christmas" was known only as the beloved hymn of Hu, a tiny, forgotten village in northern Norway, whose inhabitants spoke Huvian, a language of unknown origin. In the late 1800s, when Norwegian officials found themselves unable to communicate with the Hus, they sent for famed linguist and anthropologist Allistair McGuinn of Scotland. After many years of living with and studying the Hus, McGuinn translated many of their myths, legends, and hymns, including "Welcome Christmas." But it was not until the mid-1960s, when Dr. Seuss and Albert Hague collaborated on this partial-English translation, that this hymn became known to carolers everywhere.

Will Santy Come to Shanty Town? Page 82
(Words and Music by Eddy Arnold, Steve Nelson and Ed Nelson, Jr.)

Nashville Hall of Fame songwriter Steve Nelson, whose other works include "Peter Cottontail," "Frosty the Snow Man" and "Smokey the Bear," recalled that he was writing a number of Christmas songs in the late 1940s, when he and his brother, Ed Nelson, Jr., decided to write one about the poor boys—the boys from the other side of the tracks. Once they got the rhyme "Santy-shanty," the rest was easy, he said, but it takes a lot of feeling and sensitivity to write a lasting song like this one. Country great Eddy Arnold collaborated with the Nelsons on writing the song and later made a best-selling recording of it.

The Christmas Song

(Chestnuts Roasting on an Open Fire)

Lyric and Music by
Mel Tormé and Robert Wells

Chest-nuts roast-ing on an o-pen fire, Jack Frost nip-ping at your nose, Yule-tide car-ols be-ing sung by a choir And folks dressed up like Es-ki-mos. Ev-'ry-bod-y knows a tur-key and some

spy_____ To see if rein-deer real-ly know how to fly. *held back* And *in tempo*

so I'm of-fer-ing this sim - ple phrase To kids from one to nine-ty-

two; Al- though it's been said man-y times, man-y ways, "Mer-ry

slower Christ - mas to you."_____

Have Yourself a Merry Little Christmas

from the MGM film <u>Meet Me in St. Louis</u>
Words and Music by Hugh Martin and Ralph Blane

I'll Be Home for Christmas

Words by Kim Gannon; Music by Walter Kent

Moderately slow, in two (♩=1 beat)

L.H.
pp

C   E♭dim   Dm7   Dm7/G   G7+5

I'll   be   home   for   Christ-mas;_____
mp smoothly

C   Gm6   A7   Dm7   Edim   F6

You   can   plan   on   me.   Please   have

G7   C   Am   D7

snow   and   mis-   tle-   toe   And   pres-   ents   on   the

Christmas in Killarney

Words and Music by John Redmond,
James Cavanaugh and Frank Weldon

Irish jig tempo

The hol-ly green, the i-vy green, The pret-ti-est pic-ture you've ev-er seen Is Christ-mas in Kil-lar-ney With all of the folks at home. It's nice, you know, to kiss your beau While cud-dl-ing un-der the mis-tle-toe, And San-ta Claus you know, of course, Is one of the boys from home. The door is al-ways o-pen; The neigh-bors pay a call; And

Fa - ther John be-fore he's gone Will bless the house and all. How

grand it feels to click your heels And join in the fun of the jigs and reels; I'm

hand - ing you no blar-ney, The likes you've nev - er known *slowing down* *very slow* Is

Christ-mas in Kil-lar-ney With *in tempo* all of the folks at home. The all of the folks at home.

The Merry Christmas Polka

Words by Paul Francis Webster; Music by Sonny Burke

Moderate polka tempo

They're

tun - ing up the fid - dles now, the fid - dles now, the
round and round the room we go, the room we go, the

fid - dles now; There's wine to warm the mid - dles now, and
room we go; A - round and round the room we go, and so

1. set your head a - whirl. A-

2. get your-self a girl._____

dance   the mer - ry Christ - mas pol - ka;   An - oth - er
dance   the mer - ry Christ - mas pol - ka;   With ev - 'ry -

joy - ous   sea - son has be - gun.   Roll out the Yule - tide
bod - y   join - ing in the fun;   Roll out the bar - rels that

bar - rels   and sing out   the   car - ols,   A   mer - ry Christ - mas
cheer you,   and shout till they hear you,   A   mer - ry Christ - mas

ev - 'ry -   one!   Come on and
ev - 'ry -   one!

N.C.

Blue Christmas

Words and Music by
Billy Hayes and Jay Johnson

We Need a Little Christmas

from the musical production <u>Mame</u>
Music and Lyric by Jerry Herman

We Need a Little Christmas

THE LITTLE BOY THAT SANTA CLAUS FORGOT

Words and Music by Tommie Connor, Jimmy Leach and Michael Carr

Moderately

Verse (freely)

Christ-mas comes but once a year for ev-'ry girl and boy, The laugh-ter and the joy they find in each new toy. I'll tell you of a lit-tle boy who lives a-cross the way; This

Christmas for Cowboys

Words and Music by Steve Weisberg

CHRISTMAS IS

Words by Spence Maxwell
Music by Percy Faith

Slowly, with a lilt

Christ-mas is sleigh bells;
Christ-mas is shar-ing;

Christ-mas is hol-ly;
Christ-mas is car-ing.

ped. sim. throughout

Christ-mas is chil-dren who just can't go to sleep.
Christ-mas is car-ols to warm you in the snow;

Christ-mas is mem-'ries, the kind you al-ways keep.
Christ-mas is bed-time where no one wants to go.

Welcome Christmas
(From "How the Grinch Stole Christmas")

Music by Albert Hague; lyrics by Dr. Seuss

Take Me Back to Toyland

Words by Kal Mann; Music by Bernie Lowe

Please take me back to Toy - land;

Ev - 'ry-one's hap - py there.____ It's more than a

CHRISTMAS

Words by Jenny Lou Carson; Music by Eddy Arnold

Chorus (moderately, in tempo)

taught me to spell Christ-mas this way:

"C" is for the Christ child born up-on this day;

"H" for her-ald an-gels in the night.

"R" means our Re-deem-er; "I" means Is-ra-el;

"S" is for the star that shone so bright.

That's What I Want for Christmas

Words by Irving Caesar
Music by Gerald Marks

Make my mom-my's life a song;
I don't want e - lec-tric trains,
Keep my dad-dy safe and strong;
Twen-ty-dol-lar aer-o-planes.

Let me have them all year long;
Free our friends of aches and pains;
That's what I want for Christ-mas.
That's what I want for Christ-mas.

Let my dolls be made of rags, Fire-man hats of pa-per bags.
I like boots with tops of blue Like my lit-tle sis-ters do; So,

Just write "love" on the Christ-mas tags; That's what I want for
if you leave them,— leave a few; That's what I want for

Christ-mas. When I wake up Christ-mas day, I would
Christ-mas. When the rein-deer pass my house, I'll be

like to find a sleigh; But if I don't, dear San-ta Claus,
qui-et as a mouse. But, when I wake up, let me see

Will Santy Come to Shanty Town?

Words and Music by Eddy Arnold, Steve Nelson and Ed Nelson, Jr.

Moderately

Will San-ty come to Shan-ty Town to a poor lit-tle boy like me? Will he bring me some toys like the oth-er girls and boys? Will San-ty come to Shan-ty Town if he sees our Christ-mas tree? Mom-my said he would if I prom-ised to be

Rockin' Around the Christmas Tree

Words and Music
by Johnny Marks

*8va applies to piano only.

8va*

The Christmas Waltz

Words by Sammy Cahn; Music by Jule Styne

Gracefully, and somewhat freely

Frost-ed win-dow panes,___ can-dles gleam-ing in-side, Paint-ed

can-dy canes___ on the tree; San-ta's on his way, He's

filled his sleigh with things,___ things for you and for me. It's that

Section Three
For Children at Christmastime

Frosty the Snow Man (*Words and Music by Steve Nelson and Jack Rollins*)

Gene Autry, just out of high school and not yet settled into a job, tried to earn some money by working in a railway telegraph office in a little Oklahoma town. Assigned to the night shift, which was slow, he amused himself by picking on his guitar and singing a song or two. One night a stranger happened in, waited until Autry had finished his song and then said, "Young feller, you're wasting your time here." It was Will Rogers. By then, Autry had had enough of the telegraph business, so he took Rogers' advice and began singing professionally. His career is now legendary-he became one of Hollywood's brightest stars and ultimately earned his own radio and television shows, publishing house and even baseball team. Much of Autry's popularity came from his recordings, particularly of Christmas songs such as Steve Nelson and Jack Rollins' "Frosty the Snow Man." Autry recorded "Frosty" in 1951, and the song proved to be a million-seller. With such a send-off, it is no wonder that Frosty joined the roster of familiar characters without whom a child's Christmas can never be quite complete.

Happy Birthday, Jesus (*Words by Estelle Levitt; Music by Lee Pockriss*)

Very few Christmas songs carry a social message as does "Happy Birthday, Jesus," which manages to remain a melodic and singable work besides. Its comment on the real meaning of the holiday—that it is the birthday of Jesus—reminds us that over-commercialization distorts our values. Christmas, it says, isn't about toys and television, but about giving gifts—in this case, a song-in the spirit of the day. "Happy Birthday, Jesus" was written by popular songwriters Lee Pockriss and Estelle Levitt. Pockriss is also known as the author of such songs as "Catch a Falling Star" and "Itsy Bitsy Teenie Weenie Yellow Polka Dot Bikini."

Here Comes Santa Claus
(*Words and Music by Gene Autry and Oakley Haldeman*)

Of the several Christmas songs that contributed to Gene Autry's fame, one of them was written by The Singing Cowboy himself. That was his and Oakley Haldeman's salute to the holiday season and to one of its chief protagonists, "Here Comes Santa Claus," which he introduced in 1947. Autry's recording of the song was a sizable hit, as were the recordings by Bing Crosby and The Andrews Sisters.

Grandma Got Run Over by a Reindeer (*Words and Music by Randy Brooks*)

"'Grandma Got Run Over by a Reindeer" is a novelty Christmas song with a catchy tune that has become a perennial favorite. The song was written in 1977 by Randy Brooks, who was then a Kentucky band musician. This fun, catchy tune was originally performed by the husband and wife duo of Elmo and Patsy Shropshire in 1979. In the lyrics the grandmother of the family gets drunk from drinking too much eggnog and decides to return home to retrieve her forgotten medication. In the course of her walk, she is run over by a reindeer and is killed. The song was originally self-released by the Shropshires in 1979 on their own record label. By the early 1980s, the song had become a seasonal hit, first on country stations and then on top radio stations across the country.

A Holly Jolly Christmas (*Words and Music by Johnny Marks*)

No one wrote more Christmas musical goodies than Johnny Marks. Though well known in the popular song world, he found his true métier in writing Christmas songs, specifically "Rudolph the Red-Nosed Reindeer." After he wrote "Rudolph" in 1949, Marks set up his own company—fittingly called St. Nicholas Music Inc.—to publish the songs himself. The name of the company was a happy omen—a gift he gave himself. "Rudolph" was successful beyond Marks' wildest dreams, and he followed it with such staples as "The Night Before Christmas Song," "When Santa Claus Gets Your Letter," "Rockin' Around the Christmas Tree," "I Heard the Bells on Christmas Day" and "A Holly Jolly Christmas." The last song was premiered by Burl Ives in 1964 on the CBS children's Christmas TV special Rudolph the Red-Nosed Reindeer. *Ives' recording of "A Holly Jolly Christmas" sold more than 2 million copies.*

(All I Want for Christmas Is) My Two Front Teeth   *Page 108*
(*Words and Music by Don Gardner*)

This novelty song, which was first heard on the Perry Como radio show, was introduced coast-to-coast by a short-lived singing group called The Satisfiers. The lyrics "All I want for Christmas is my two front teeth," supposedly sung by a lisping child, delighted Como's audience and led to a 1948 smash recording by musical madcap Spike Jones. Written in 1946 by Don Gardner, the song still generates a chuckle today.

The Night Before Christmas Song   *Page 116*
(*Words by Clement Clarke Moore, adapted by Johnny Marks; Music by Johnny Marks*)

Clement Clarke Moore was one of 19th-century America's most distinguished scholars in the fields of Oriental and Greek literature. He achieved fame far beyond what might be expected for even so eminent a scholar, and that fame has proved enduring. It rests not on his research, however, but on the charm of a simple poem that he wrote at the age of 42 to entrance his six children on Christmas Eve. He called it "A Visit from St. Nicholas," and it started with the magic sentence "'Twas the night before Christmas," the title by which his poem is now commonly known. Johnny Marks, who wrote so many of our popular Christmas tunes, adapted Moore's poem into a song.

Nuttin' for Christmas (*Words and Music by Sid Tepper and Roy C. Bennett*)   *Page 113*

Co-writers Sid Tepper and Roy Bennett have had amazingly parallel careers. Both were born the same year, served in the Air Force Special Services during World War II, were staff writers for Mills Music and wrote special material for Elvis Presley—and had lots of children. It was one of Bennett's daughters, Claire, who inspired this charming song—like the child in the song, she spilled some ink on Mommy's rug and was warned that the impending Christmas would be a bleak one. Each writer contributed mischievous incidents from his own family, and the result was "Nuttin' for Christmas." Five-year-old Barry Gordon introduced the song on The Milton Berle Show *in the mid-1950s. That appearance was so successful that renditions by Stan Freberg, Eartha Kitt, and Homer and Jethro quickly followed.*

Rudolph the Red-Nosed Reindeer (*Words and Music by Johnny Marks*)   *Page 91*

The statistics are staggering: more than 160 million recordings by more than 500 different performers and some 7 million copies of sheet music, not to mention toys, clothing, watches, all bearing the image of a shiny-nosed deer. The cause of it all? "Rudolph the Red-Nosed Reindeer" by Johnny Marks, one of the most successful songs of all time. Cowboy star Gene Autry introduced "Rudolph" at Madison Square Garden in New York City in 1949. His recording has since sold more than 12 of those 160 million recordings, a half-million in 1980 alone—making it the second biggest-selling recording after Bing Crosby's version of "White Christmas." "Rudolph" has inspired several television specials, and the little reindeer is still a popular favorite every Christmas, joining Dancer and Prancer and the other six reindeer around Santa's sleigh.

Santa Claus, Indiana, U.S.A.   *Page 118*
(*Words and Music by Abe Olman and Al Jacobs*)

There actually is a town called Santa Claus in the state of Indiana—a little town of about 1,200 people, where many of the letters that children address to Santa Claus every year eventually wind up. This song, written from the point of view of a child, gives the idea a little twist: he would answer any lost letters addressed to Santa and would mail Daddy and Mommy's Christmas gift from the town. Abe Olman's most popular song is "Oh! Johnny Oh!," which he wrote in 1917. Al Jacobs wrote most of his popular songs, which included "This is My Country," during the 1930s and '40s.

Section Three: For Children at Christmastime

Everybody knows what happens if you pout or cry around Christmastime: Santa Claus passes you by, that's what. Haven Gillespie and J. Fred Coots wrote words and music to this effect in 1932, but no music publisher was interested in the song because it was a "kiddie" tune and "kiddie" tunes were "known" to be "uncommercial." At the time Coots was writing special material for comedian Eddie Cantor, to whom he showed the song. But even Cantor was about to turn it down for his radio show until his wife Ida persuaded him to give it a try—this was near Thanksgiving in 1934—and of course it was an instantaneous hit. The radio audience went wild over the song, everybody bought the sheet music, and another Christmas standard was born. Since then there have been many recordings of "Santa Claus Is Comin' to Town," but the ones by Bing Crosby and The Andrews Sisters and Perry Como were the most successful.

"Suzy Snowflake" has been a children's doll, a three-minute animated cartoon and a popular song. Of the three, the song proved to be the least ephemeral. Penned by longtime collaborators Sid Tepper and Roy C. Bennett, it was dedicated to Tepper's baby daughter, Susan. During their long career together, Tepper and Bennett have written a number of memorable songs, including "Nuttin' for Christmas," "Red Roses for a Blue Lady," "Say Something Sweet to Your Sweetheart" and "The Naughty Lady of Shady Lane."

Although "Thirty-Two Feet and Eight Little Tails" never quite matched the popularity of the beloved "Rudolph the Red-Nosed Reindeer," it nevertheless became a favorite in the recording lineup of America's favorite singing cowboy, Gene Autry. Designed to bring Christmas cheer to young and old alike, its lyrics sing of Santa's hurried ride through the night with his eight little reindeer.

Babes in Toyland, *one of Victor Herbert's enchanting operettas, written in 1903, proved that the master could write children's entertainments as well as he could sentimental love stories, which meant better than almost anyone else in those turn-of-the-century days. Toward the beginning of the evening, which includes a breathtaking Christmas pageant as well as such songs as "I Can't Do the Sum" and "March of the Toys," the toys all join in a tribute to their fabulous country, "Toyland." One reviewer called* **Babes in Toyland** *a "perfect dream of delight," and another, praising the ingenious scenery, rich costumes and dazzling music, wrote, "What more could the spirit of mortal desire?" The song "Toyland" casts a nostalgic, almost hypnotic spell with its swaying innocent rhythm.*

Clement Clarke Moore's poem "A Visit from St. Nicholas," written in 1822 and now more familiarly known by its first line, " 'Twas the night before Christmas," clarified for many children and their parents the exact fashion in which Santa Claus paid his visits—what he looked like, what the names of his reindeer were, how he got himself down the chimney. "Up on the Housetop," which was written in the mid-19th century by an Ohioan, Benjamin Russell Hanby, probably owes something to "A Visit from St. Nicholas," since no one before Moore had suggested that Santa's sleigh could land on a rooftop at all.

This was a hit song that was inspired by another hit song. Songwriter Johnny Marks recalled that after Gene Autry recorded "Rudolph the Red-Nosed Reindeer," which became such a hit in 1949, The New York Times was swamped with letters from children who had written to Santa Claus asking for a copy of the Rudolph record for Christmas. Those charming letters gave Marks the idea for "When Santa Claus Gets Your Letter." Autry recorded that song, too, and it also became a hit, though not, of course, as big a hit as "Rudolph."

Rudolph the Red-Nosed Reindeer

Words and Music by Johnny Marks

Thirty-Two Feet and Eight Little Tails

(Dasher, Dancer, Prancer, Vixen, Comet, Cupid, Donner, Blitzen)

Words and Music by John Redmond, James Cavanaugh and Frank Weldon

Here Comes Santa Claus

Words and Music by Gene Autry and Oakley Haldeman

Here comes San-ta Claus, Here comes San-ta Claus Right down San-ta Claus Lane.
Here comes San-ta Claus, Here comes San-ta Claus Right down San-ta Claus Lane.

Vix-en and Blitz-en and all his rein-deer are pull-ing on the rein.
He does-n't care if you're rich or poor for he loves you just the same.

Bells are ring-ing, chil-dren sing-ing; All is mer-ry and bright.
San-ta knows that we're God's chil-dren; That makes ev-'ry-thing right.

Santa Claus Is Comin' to Town

Words and Music by
J. Fred Coots and Haven Gillespie

Moderately, with a lilt

No chords

mp throughout

Organ: No pedal

You bet-ter watch out; you bet-ter not cry;

Bet-ter not pout; I'm tell-ing you why: San-ta Claus is com-in' to

town. He's mak-ing a list and check-ing it twice;

Gon-na find out who's naugh-ty and nice: San-ta Claus is com-in' to

Pianists play a quarter note here.

A HOLLY JOLLY CHRISTMAS

Words and Music by Johnny Marks

WHEN SANTA CLAUS GETS YOUR LETTER

Words and Music by Johnny Marks

Gaily

When San-ta Claus gets your let-ter, you know what he will say: "Have
(2) San-ta Claus gets your let-ter to ask for Christ-mas toys, He'll

you been good the way you should on ev-'ry sin-gle day?" 2. When
take a look in his good book he keeps for girls and boys. He'll stroke his beard, his eyes will glow, and

up on the housetop

Words and Music by Benjamin Russell Hanby

Gaily

F

(sing as written; play 8va higher)

Bb   F   C⁷₄   C7

1. Up on the house-top__ rein-deer pause; Out jumps good old San-ta Claus,
2. First comes the stock-ing of lit-tle Nell; Oh, dear San-ta, fill it well;
3. Look in the stock-ing of lit-tle Bill; Oh, just see that glo-rious fill!

mp

No organ pedals until last note

F   Bb   F

(1) Down through the chim-ney with lots of toys, All for the lit-tle ones'
(2) Give her a dol-ly that laughs and cries, One that can o-pen and
(3) Here is a ham-mer and lots of tacks, Whis-tle and ball and a

C⁷₄   C7   F   Bb   Am7   D7   Gm7   C⁷₄   F

Chorus

(1) Christ-mas joys.
(2) shut its eyes. Ho, ho, ho, who would-n't go? Ho, ho, ho, who would-n't go?__
(3) set of jacks.

F   F7   Bb   F   Bdim   F   Gm7   C7   F

D.C.

Up on the house-top, click, click, click, Down through the chim-ney with good Saint Nick.

104

Frosty the Snow Man

Words and Music by
Steve Nelson and Jack Rollins

Moderately

pp cresc.

Fros - ty the Snow Man was a jol - ly, hap - py soul, With a
Fros - ty the Snow Man knew the sun was hot that day, So he

corn - cob pipe and a but - ton nose and two eyes made out of coal.
said, "Let's run and we'll have some fun now be - fore I melt a - way."

Fros - ty the Snow Man is a fair - y tale, they say; He was
Down to the vil - lage with a broom - stick in his hand, Run - ning

Frosty the Snow Man

made of snow, but the chil-dren know how he came to life one day. There
here and there all a-round the square, say-in', "Catch me if you can." He
more

must have been some mag-ic in that old silk hat they found, For
led them down the streets of town right to the traf-fic cop, And he
broadly

when they placed it on his head, he be-gan to dance a-
on-ly paused a mo-ment when he heard him hol-ler,

round. Oh, Fros-ty the Snow Man was a-live as he could
"Stop!" For Fros-ty the Snow Man had to hur-ry on his
as before

(All I Want for Christmas Is)
My Two Front Teeth

Words and Music by Don Gardner

Suzy Snowflake

Words and Music by Sid Tepper and Roy C. Bennett

Here comes Suzy Snowflake, Dressed in a snow-white gown,
Here comes Suzy Snowflake; Soon you will hear her say,
Tap, tap, tappin' at your window-pane To tell you she's in town.
"Come out ev'ry-one and play with me; I haven't long to stay.

If you wan-na make a snow-man, I'll help you make one, one, two, three.

If you wan-na take a sleigh ride, The ride's on me."

Here comes Su-zy Snow-flake; Look at her tum-blin' down,

Bring-ing joy to ev-'ry girl and boy; Su-zy's come to town.

Su - zy's come to town.

Toyland

Words by Glen MacDonough; Music by Victor Herbert

Gently

Toy - land, Toy - land, Lit - tle girl and boy land,

While you dwell with -in it____ You are ev - er hap - py then.

Child - hood's joy - land, Mys - tic, mer - ry Toy - land!

Once you pass its bor - ders, You can ne'er__ re-turn a - gain.____

*Note: Guitarists tune lowest string ½ tone higher to F.

NUTTIN' FOR CHRISTMAS

Words and Music by Sid Tepper and Roy C. Bennett

The Night Before Christmas Song

Words by Clement Clarke Moore, adapted by Johnny Marks; Music by Johnny Marks

Santa Claus, Indiana, U.S.A.

Words and Music by Abe Olman and Al Jacobs

good lit-tle girls and boys, Say-ing San-ta will bring your toys. With eight rein-deer he'll ap-pear, rid-ing on a sleigh. Then I'd mail *lightly* Dad-dy's and Mom-my's sur-prise for Christ-mas Day, From San-ta Claus, In-di-an-a, U. S., San-ta Claus, In-di-an-a, U. S., San-ta Claus, In-di-an-a, U. S. A.

Grandma Got Run Over By a Reindeer

Words and Music by Randy Brooks

Dm

19

When   we   found   her   Christ-mas   morn-ing
It's   not   Christ-mas   with-out   Grand-ma,
I've   warned   all   my   friends   and   neigh-bors,

Am

C7

21

at   the   scene   of   the   at   -   tack,
all   the   fam   -   'ly's   dressed   in   black.
bet   -   ter   watch   out   for   your   -   selves.

F

F7

23

she   had   foot-prints   on   her   fore-head,   and   in -
And   we   just   can't   help   but   won   -   der: Should we
They   should   nev   -   er   give   a   li   -   cense   To   a

Bb

C7

25

crim   -   i   -   nat   -   ing   Claus   marks   on   her   back.
o   -   pen   up   her   gifts   or   send   them   back?
man   who   drives   a   sleigh   and   plays   with   elves.

F

Play 3 times

Coda

27   No chords

p ————————————— *ff*

122

Happy Birthday, Jesus

Words by Estelle Levitt; Music by Lee Pockriss

(1) Mom–ma stayed up all night long,   Sit-ting in the kitch-en
(2) ev–'ry–bod–y's gift was gone,   I still had my pres-ent;
(3) an–y-thing that's on T V,   Some-thing ver-y spe-cial,

(1) mak-ing us a pres-ent;   it was this song:
(2) Mom–ma's song of Christ-mas   lived on and on:
(3) some-thing made for-ev-er,   this mel-o-dy:

Chorus

Church bells ring-a-ling, an-gels sing-a-ling;   "Hap-py Birth-day, Je-sus."
sim.

Snow-flakes ting-a-ling, sleigh bells jing-a-ling;   "Hap-py Birth-day, Je-sus."

Happy Birthday, Jesus

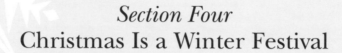

Section Four
Christmas Is a Winter Festival

Everyone knows Meredith Willson as the composer of The Music Man, *a smash Broadway hit in 1957. Before that, however, he had already achieved two of his biggest musical successes. One was in connection with Tallulah Bankhead. Willson conducted her radio program* The Big Show, *and wrote for her its closing signature tune, "May the Good Lord Bless and Keep You." (He also became known as the comical man who embarrassedly addressed the baritone-voiced actress as "Miss Bankhead, sir.") That was in 1950. The following year his warmly melodic song "It's Beginning to Look Like Christmas" was one of the hits of the season. He wrote both the music and text, with the message that the carol you sing in your heart is the loveliest Christmas music of all.*

In 1950, Walt Disney produced a true-life adventure film, Beaver Valley, *for which Paul Smith wrote the background music and collaborated with Don Raye on the songs, including "Jing-A-Ling, Jing-A-Ling." Smith, who was associated with a number of Disney films, was a Juilliard graduate. Raye came from much humbler musical origins, and during the 1920s danced and sang in vaudeville. Both a composer and lyricist, he has a number of classic songs to his credit, including "Beat Me Daddy, Eight to the Bar," "This Is My Country," "I'll Remember April" and "Boogie Woogie Bugle Boy."*

Though, for most of us, "Jingle Bells" has come to be practically synonymous with Christmas, James Pierpont wrote it in 1857 for a Thanksgiving program at the large Boston church where he taught Sunday school. He titled his song "The One Horse Open Sleigh" and made the rhythm so jaunty and the words so catchy that his 40 little Sunday schoolers learned it almost instantaneously. (A friend of Pierpont's admiring the song, called it a "merry little jingle" and helped give the tune the name by which we know it today.) The children's first performance was such a success that they were asked to repeat it at Christmastime, whereupon the sleigh apparently took on the identity of Santa's sled, and "Jingle Bells" became a Christmas song forever.

"Jingle-Bell Rock" has nothing to do with James Pierpont's 1857 song "Jingle Bells." It was written exactly a century later, when rock 'n' roll was coming on strong and casting its new rhythmic vitality over everything, including the Christmas season. Joe Beal, a New England-born public relations man, collaborated with Jim Boothe, a Texas writer in the advertising business, to create this unique novelty, which became a best-selling record for singer Bobby Helms.

Let It Snow! Let It Snow! Let It Snow!
(*Words by Sammy Cahn; Music by Jule Styne*)

Page 134

Blend the lyrics of Sammy Cahn with the music of Jule Styne and you're bound to get a ballad that will make history. In the one year of 1944, this pair turned out "I Fall in Love Too Easily," "I'll Walk Alone" and "Saturday Night (Is the Loneliest Night in the Week)." Then, the next year had barely started when they produced the wintertime classic "Let It Snow! Let It Snow! Let It Snow!"—which was turned into an immediate hit recording by Vaughn Monroe. "Let It Snow!" offers a choice between the bitter weather outside and a crackling warm fire inside. Any difficulty in making your choice?

A Marshmallow World (*Words by Carl Sigman; Music by Peter De Rose*)

Page 136

Peter De Rose, who also wrote the lushly romantic "Deep Purple" and the inspirational "I Heard a Forest Praying," turned to another facet of his talent for the sparkling melody of "A Marshmallow World." Carl Sigman contributed a delicious lyric about what makes a white Christmas white—though it may seem to be all marshmallows and whipped cream, it's actually a blanket of fresh snow, with more flakes falling all the time. De Rose's song gave a lift to the Christmas of 1949, and Bing Crosby's recording of it was the most successful of several contenders.

Over the River and Through the Woods (*Traditional*)

Page 142

At one time, "Over the River and Through the Woods" was a favorite song of the Thanksgiving season. It detailed the delights of a sleigh ride to Grandmother's house and the goodies that would be found there by children and adults alike. But over the years, this jolly tune, which probably dates from the 1870s, has come to be associated with Christmas instead. In an old book of carols, there exists a published version of the song that dates back to 1897 and bears the name "Edw. Trotter, Rev." as composer, but the attribution is somewhat suspect. The book also includes "The First Noël," and the Reverend Mr. Trotter also listed himself as composer of that carol and of several other traditional tunes in the collection. Nevertheless, "Over the River" must have been familiar enough that members of Trotter's congregation would have forgotten its actual composer and been willing to accept their preacher's word that he wrote it. (Or, possibly, he did!)

Sleigh Ride (*Words by Mitchell Parish; Music by Leroy Anderson*)

Page 138

Leroy Anderson's "Sleigh Ride" has the brisk charm of a winter scene in some Currier and Ives print, the horse-drawn sleigh moving gaily over the snow to the sound of sleigh bells and the occasional crack of a whip. It has become a Christmastime classic, although Anderson claimed he composed it in the midst of a sweltering August heat wave in 1948. (Mitchell Parish added lyrics to Anderson's tune two years later.) The song was first performed by Arthur Fiedler and The Boston Pops Orchestra, for whom Anderson was an arranger, and was such a success with its clip-clops and bells and horse whinnies that it had to be repeated immediately for the audience. "Sleigh Ride," like most Anderson compositions–"The Typewriter" and "The Syncopated Clock" among them—is as American as apple pie, as popular as hot dogs.

Section Four: Christmas Is a Winter Festival

Winter (*Words by Alfred Bryan; Music by Albert Gumble*)

The lyrics to "Winter" were written by Canadian-born Alfred Bryan in 1910, the same year that he wrote "Come, Josephine, in My Flying Machine," and both songs reflect the naïve charm of pre–World War I Tin Pan Alley. Bryan's best-known song is the perennial favorite "Peg o' My Heart." Albert Gumble, composer and pianist noted for his contributions to vaudeville, was one of Bryan's many collaborators, and together they penned "Are You Sincere?" and "Winter." Both men were charter members of the American Society of Composers, Authors and Publishers (ASCAP).

Winter Wonderland (*Words by Dick Smith; Music by Felix Bernard*)

Felix Bernard, the composer of "Winter Wonderland," also co-wrote the melody of the 1919 hit "Dardanella." (The recording by Ben Selvin's Novelty Orchestra is believed to be the first in history to sell one million copies.) Fifteen years later he teamed up with Dick Smith on "Winter Wonderland," an immediate hit for Guy Lombardo and His Royal Canadians. Then, in 1946, rival recordings were made by Perry Como and The Andrews Sisters (backed by Guy Lombardo) that established the bubbly tune as a Yuletide favorite. The song has since been recorded hundreds of times for Christmas albums by everyone from the pop group Air Supply to Broadway star Karen Ziemba.

IT'S BEGINNING TO LOOK LIKE CHRISTMAS

Words and Music by Meredith Willson

Moderately, with a lilt

It's be -
(2. (It's be-) gin-ning to look a lot like Christ-mas

Ev - 'ry-where you

go;_____

go;_____

Take a look in the five - and-ten,

There's a tree in the Grand Ho-tel,

It's Beginning to Look Like Christmas

glis-ten-ing once a-gain
one in the park as well,

With
The

can-dy canes and sil-ver lanes a-
stur-dy kind that does-n't mind the

glow._____
snow._____

It's be-gin-ning to look a lot like Christ-mas,
It's be-gin-ning to look a lot like Christ-mas;

Toys in ev-'ry store,_____
Soon the bells will start,_____

But the pret-ti-est sight to see is the
And the thing that will make them ring is the

hol-ly that will be On your own front door. A pair of
car-ol that you sing Right with-

To Patter

130

Last ending

in your heart.

Patter

hop-a-long boots and a pis-tol that shoots Is the wish of Bar-ney and Ben;

Dolls that will talk and will go for a walk Is the hope of Jan-ice and Jen; And

D.S. to last ending

Mom and Dad can hard-ly wait for school to start a-gain. 2. It's be-

Jingle Bells

**Words and Music
by James Pierpont**

Gaily

Dash-ing through the snow   In a one-horse o-pen sleigh,

O'er the fields we go,   Laugh-ing all the way.

Bells on bob-tail ring,   Mak-ing spir-its bright;   What

*8va applies to piano only.

8va*

Let It Snow!

A Marshmallow World

Words by Carl Sigman; Music by Peter De Rose

Sleigh Ride

Words by Mitchell Parish; Music by Leroy Anderson

Note: For an optional effect between [A] and [B] and between [C] and [D], you might call on a "third hand" to imitate sleigh bells by playing as follows on the high side of the keyboard—

Just hear those sleigh bells jin-gl-ing, ring-ting-tin-gl-ing, too;___ ___Come on, it's love-ly weath-er for a sleigh ride to-geth-er with you.___

Sleigh Ride

Over the River and Through the Woods

Traditional

Brightly, in one (♩.=1 beat)

1. O-ver the riv-er and through the woods To Grand-moth-er's house we
2. O-ver the riv-er and through the woods To have a full day of
3. O-ver the riv-er and through the woods And straight through the barn-yard

(1) go. The horse knows the way to car-ry the sleigh Through
(2) play. Oh, hear the bells ring-ing ting-a-ling-ling, For
(3) gate. It seems that we go so dread-ful-ly slow; It

Winter Wonderland

Words by Dick Smith; Music by Felix Bernard

Moderately, with a lilt

Sleigh-bells ring, are you lis-t'nin'? In the lane, snow is
way is the blue-bird, here to stay

glis-t'nin', A beau-ti-ful sight,__ we're hap-py to-night,__
new bird, He sings a love song,__ as we go a-long,__

Walk-in' in a win-ter won-der-land! Gone a-
Walk-in' in a win-ter won-der-land!

In the mea - dow we can build a snow - man,

Then pre - tend that he is Par - son Brown;

He'll say, "Are you mar - ried?" We'll say, "No man! But

you can do the job when you're in town!" La - ter

Jingle-Bell Rock

**Words and Music by
Joe Beal and Jim Boothe**

With a light swing

Jin-gle-bell, jin-gle-bell, jin-gle-bell rock,— Jin-gle bells swing— and

jin-gle bells ring. Snow-in' and blow-in' up bush-els of fun,

Now the jin-gle hop has be-gun.— Jin-gle-bell, jin-gle-bell, jin-gle-bell rock,— Jin-gle bells chime in jin-gle-bell time.

Danc-in' and pranc-in' in Jin-gle Bell Square In the frost-y air.—

What a bright— time;— it's the right— time— To rock the night a-

way. Jin-gle- bell— time— is a swell time— To go glid-in' in a

Winter

Words by Alfred Bryan
Music by Albert Gumble

and De-cem-ber, just re-mem-ber Win - ter, win - ter, When your sweet-heart comes a - call - ing, By the fire - side so bright, you'll sit and tease her; That's the time to squeeze her, when it's win - ter.

Words by Don Raye
Music by Paul J. Smith

Jing-A-Ling, Jing-A-Ling

Bright polka tempo

p cresc. (like approaching sleigh bells) *f*

Jing, jing-a-ling, jing-a-ling, jing-a-ling, What fun to hear the
Jing, jing-a-ling, jing-a-ling, jing-a-ling, The bells have got the

sleigh bells jin - gle. Jing, jing-a-ling, jing-a- ling, jing-a-ling, They
snow-flakes danc - ing. Jing, jing-a-ling, jing-a- ling, jing-a-ling, Ol'

set your heart a - tin - gle. Jing, jing-a-ling, jing-a-
Dob - bin's e - ven pranc - ing. Jing, jing-a-ling, jing-a-

152

ling, jing-a-ling, I love to hear our laugh-ter min-gle, Ha, ha,
ling, jing-a-ling, The night is made for sweet ro-manc-ing. Ha, ha,

ho, ho, glid - ing through the snow.
ho, ho, through the snow we

go.

Through a
non-legato

Trio

win - ter fair-y - land we go a - glid - ing_____ In a

Section Five
Modern Carols

Carol of the Bells *(Words by Peter J. Wilhousky; Music by M. Leontovich)*   *Page 164*

There is a legend that at the stroke of midnight on the evening when Jesus was born all the bells on earth suddenly began pealing joyously together of their own accord—and there was never a sound like it for majesty and grandeur. "Carol of the Bells," based on an old Ukrainian motif, probably springs from that legend, as it tells of the "sweet silver bells" that pealed joyously in unison. Traditionally, the "Carol of the Bells" is sung quietly in the beginning, grows louder and ever louder as each voice adds to the tintinnabulation, and finally dies away to a pianissimo as the pealing gradually ceases.

I Heard the Bells on Christmas Day   *Page 160*
(Words by Henry Wadsworth Longfellow, adapted by Johnny Marks;
Music by Johnny Marks)

A mood of intense melancholy overtook poet Henry Wadsworth Longfellow in the years after his wife's tragic death in a fire in 1861. The Civil War had broken out that same year, and it seemed to him that this was an additional punishment. Sitting down at his desk one day, he penned the poem "Christmas Bells." As the bells continue to peal and peal, Longfellow recognizes that God is not dead after all, that right shall prevail, bringing peace and goodwill, as long as there is Christmas and its promise of new life. The poem has been sung to a tune written in the 1870s by an English organist, John Baptiste Calkin. In the 1950s, Johnny Marks, whose Christmas songs are many and choice, adapted Longfellow's words and provided the modern musical setting that is used here and is commonly sung today. There have been many recordings of Marks' version, including ones by Kate Smith, Frank Sinatra, Harry Belafonte and Bing Crosby (who joked to Marks, "I see you finally got yourself a decent lyricist").

The Little Drummer Boy   *Page 162*
(Words and Music by Katherine Davis, Henry Onorati and Harry Simeone)

Harry Simeone, who was at one time choral conductor-assistant to Fred Waring, wrote what is now a Christmas classic, "The Little Drummer Boy," in 1958. The song tells the story of a shepherd boy who makes his way along with the procession of the Wise Men and other admirers to the lowly manger in Bethlehem to see the Holy Babe. Some of those who gather at the manger present the Infant with fine gifts, but all the shepherd has to offer is his drum and his gift of making music. The whole carol is accompanied by a gentle drone, the sound of the boy's drum being played lightly with the fingers. The Harry Simeone Chorale made the best-selling recording of its leader's song.

Out of the East *(Words and Music by Harry Noble)*   *Page 157*

Juilliard-trained songwriter Harry Noble wrote "Out of the East" in 1940. The song describes the trip of the Magi, following the star to the birthplace of Jesus, and is an inspiring song of faith. Noble, born in New York and raised in Jersey City, New Jersey, was best known for his song "Hold Me, Thrill Me, Kiss Me." In addition to directing a prize-winning girls' choir, he was a nightclub performer with Francis King for many years, appeared in films, and gave organ lessons at Bamberger's Department Store in Newark, New Jersey.

The Peace Carol *(Words and Music by Bob Beers)*   *Page 166*

The Beers of upstate New York were a musical family reminiscent of the famous Trapp family of Vermont. In 1965, they had several pleasant visits with the Reverend Edith Craig Reynolds, a Baptist minister related by marriage to the Reynolds Aluminum family. Bob Beers was so inspired by the gentle wisdom of Reverend Reynolds that he wrote this carol in her honor. The theme is a simple one—that the grief and struggles and cares of the world can be overcome by the peace of Christmas Day.

Words and Music by Harry Noble

Out of the East

Moderately

1. Out of the East there came rid-ing, rid-ing, Three of the wis-est of
2. In-to the West they went rid-ing, rid-ing, Fol-low-ing af-ter the
3. Lo! in a man-ger they found Him, found Him, Bathed in the light of yon

I Heard the Bells on Christmas Day

Words by Henry Wadsworth Longfellow,
adapted by Johnny Marks; Music by Johnny Marks

Rapidly, in one (♩. = 1 beat)

Slowly

G   Gaug   C/E   D7   Em   F#   Bm

heard the bells on Christ-mas Day Their old fa - mil - iar car - ols play, And

Cm/E♭   D7   Dm/F   E7   C   E7   Fdim   A9/E   D7

wild and sweet the words re-peat Of peace on earth, good- will to men. I

cresc.

G   Gaug   C/E   D7   Em   F#   Bm

thought as now this day had come, The bel - fries of all Chris - ten - dom Had

The Little Drummer Boy

Words and Music by
Katherine Davis, Henry Onorati
and Harry Simeone

Moderately, in two (♩ = 1 beat)

Guitar → D
(Capo up
3 frets)

Keyboard → F

1. Come, they told me, (Pa-
2. Lit - tle Ba - by, (Pa-
   (Ba - by Ge - su),
3. Mar - y nod - ded; (Pa-

p throughout

(Bells)

(1) rum-pum-pum-pum)____ A new-born King to see; (Pa-
(2) rum-pum-pum-pum)____ I am a poor boy too; (Pa-
(3) rum-pum-pum-pum)____ The ox and lamb kept time; (Pa-

(1) rum-pum-pum-pum)____ Our fin-est gifts we bring (Pa-
(2) rum-pum-pum-pum)____ I have no gift to bring (Pa-
(3) rum-pum-pum-pum)____ I played my drum for Him; (Pa-

Carol of the Bells

Words by Peter J. Wilhousky; Music by M. Leontovich

Joyfully, in one (each measure = 1 beat)

Hark! how the bells, | Sweet sil-ver bells, | All seem to say, | "Throw cares a-way."

Christ-mas is here, | Bring-ing good cheer | To young and old, | Meek and the bold.

Ding, dong, ding, dong, | That is their song | With joy-ful ring, | All car-ol-ing.

One seems to hear | Words of good cheer | From ev-'ry-where | Fill-ing the air; | O

*Guitarists: Play chords finger style.

The Peace Carol

Words and Music by Bob Beers

Gently

mp

1. The

G   Gaug   C/G

(1) gar - ment of life   be it   tat - tered and torn,   The
(2) hope that has slum - bered for   two thou - sand years,   A
3. Add all the grief __ that peo - ple may bear; __

F/G   D7/G   G   Em   Em/D

(1) cloak of the sol - dier is   weath-ered and worn, But what Child is this that was
(2) prom-ise that si-lenced a   thou - sand fears, A faith that can hob - ble   an
(3) To - tal the strife and the   trou - ble and care; __ Put them in col - umns and

A/C♯   D7   G

(1) pov - er - ty - born? The peace of Christ - mas Day. __
(2) o - cean of   tears, The peace of Christ - mas Day. __ } The branch that bears the
(3) leave them right there, The peace of Christ - mas Day. __

166

Section Six
Favorite Carols of Yesterday and Today

Angels from the Realms of Glory   *Page 174*
(Words by James Montgomery; Music by Henry Smart)

In the mid-1790s, 23-year-old James Montgomery, a devout Moravian newspaperman in Sheffield, England, was twice imprisoned because authorities feared that his liberalism and criticism of local officials might breed trouble. He took advantage of his incarceration to write a little book, Prison Amusements, *which he published as soon as he was released and had returned to his newspaper. The success of the book started him and his paper, the* Iris, *on the road to such popularity that before long he became one of Sheffield's leading citizens. His Christian faith, so strong in adversity, remained just as strong in prosperity. He published many hymns, including "Angels from the Realms of Glory," which he wrote for the Christmas Eve edition of the Iris in 1816, and which was republished in the* Christian Psalmist *in 1825. Some years later, a London organist, Henry Smart, wrote the music to which we now sing Montgomery's words.*

As Lately We Watched *(Traditional)*   *Page 181*

From Austria comes this traditional carol, sung to a tune similar to the old English "We Wish You a Merry Christmas." As with such other carols as "Angels We Have Heard on High," "Angels from the Realms of Glory" and "While Shepherds Watched Their Flocks by Night," the song tells the story of the Nativity from the point of view of the shepherds near Bethlehem who follow the path of the star, hear the angels proclaim the birth of the newborn King and finally see the Infant in His manger-throne.

As with Gladness Men of Old   *Page 189*
(Words by William Chatterton Dix; Music by Conrad Kocher)

On the Epiphany, the Twelfth Day of Christmas, probably in 1858, William Chatterton Dix was sick in bed. Dix was a devout churchman who ran a marine insurance company in England during the week and composed hymns on Sunday. While sick, he managed to read the Gospel for the day, which inspired him to write this classic Christmas hymn. It was set to a melody written several decades earlier by an eminent German organist, Conrad Kocher, but Dix is often credited with the tune. Dix eventually came to dislike his abridgment of the Kocher setting, but realized that since the combination of words and music had already entered the literature it was too late to change it.

Christians, Awake, Salute the Happy Morn   *Page 178*
(Words by John Byrom; Music by John Wainwright)

This song was written by John Byrom as a Christmas present for his daughter, probably in 1749. Byrom was active in the evangelical revivals of the period, had both Charles and John Wesley as students and friends, and ended life as a Quaker. The poem was first published as a broadside (broadsides were large sheets of paper on which ballads were customarily printed, and which were sold by stationers like newspapers) and was set to an original psalm tune, "Yorkshire" by John Wainwright, an organist at the Manchester, England, Collegiate Church. Byrom first heard the completed hymn on Christmas Day, 1750, when a group of men and boys led by Wainwright sang it for him.

Good Christian Men, Rejoice   *Page 184*
(Words by John Mason Neale; Music Traditional)

This well-worked melody served a variety of purposes before it became the setting for "Good Christian Men, Rejoice." Its origin is a 14th-century hymn, which was arranged in 1601 by Bartholomaeus Gesius as "In Dulci Jubilo." Subsequently Johann Sebastian Bach made his own arrangement of the melody in his Chorale Preludes for the organ, and in an edition by Sir John Stainer, it became well known to German-speaking people as "Nun singet und seid froh." The English version is by the Reverend Dr. John Mason Neale, a 19th-century English minister who, after being forced into retirement by illness, collected and made English translations of many Greek and Latin hymns.

The Holly and the Ivy *(Traditional)* *Page 180*

The verses of this charming English carol date back centuries. They were first officially published in 1861 by a Joshua Sylvester, who admitted that he had obtained them from "an old broadside, printed a century and a half since." The symbolism in them probably pre-dates Christianity and was simply modified to serve it. Hence, the white blossoms became the purity of Mary; the red berries, Jesus' blood; the thorns, His crown; the bitter bark, His crucifixion agony. The symbolism of the ivy has been lost, although some suggest that the holly stands for the masculine elements of Jesus' birth, and the clinging ivy for the feminine elements.

I Saw Three Ships *(Traditional)* *Page 171*

There are several interpretations of the three ships mentioned in this carol. Since the music was published for the first time in 1666, less than two centuries after Columbus's voyages had opened up the seas, some believe that the three ships, like Columbus's, were entering a New World – that of the Spirit. Others feel that the number refers to the journeying Wise Men, or to the virtues of faith, hope and charity, or to the Holy Family of Jesus, Mary and Joseph, or to the Trinity of God the Father, Son and Holy Spirit. Carols that sing of ships are not usual, though as Cecil Sharp, a famous collector of folk songs, pointed out, the island-dwelling Britons of early days may have thought that Bethlehem, which they knew about only through hearsay, lay on or near the seacoast of the Holy Land. Sharp discovered the music for this carol existing in similar versions all over the British Isles, sung to these Christmas words and also to a secular lyric, beginning "As I sat on a sunny bank," which was already well known by the 18th century.

Joseph Dearest, Joseph Mild *(Traditional)* *Page 176*

"Joseph Dearest, Joseph Mild" is a lullaby that was sung by the Virgin Mary in a Mystery Play that flourished around Leipzig, Germany, in the early 1500s. The tune was originally sung to a Latin text full of joy, "Resonet in Laudibus" (Let Our Praises Resound), dating from as early as the 14th century. Before that time, carols and other religious songs were danced and sung to primitive tunes and graceless texts. But a new awareness of beauty in worship swept through Europe in the 1500s, thanks in part to the Reformation, and melodies took on an ingratiating texture, while texts issued from the pens of genius poets.

Lo, How a Rose E'er Blooming *(Traditional; arranged by Dan Fox)* *Page 175*

This charming old carol comes to us from Germany's Rhineland. It was first published in 1599 in Cologne but could date from the 15th century or perhaps even earlier. Michael Praetorius harmonized it in 1609, and Theodore Baker, the American music scholar who first compiled the Biographical Dictionary of Musicians *in 1900, is credited with the English translation. In some hymnals, the carol appears as "I Know a Rose-Tree Springing" or "Behold a Branch Is Growing" from its original German text, "Es ist ein' Ros' entsprungen."*

O Come, O Come Emmanuel *(Traditional)* *Page 186*

The words to this church hymn for the season of Advent are very old indeed. They were of such importance in medieval days that in monasteries a separate stanza, to be sung from December 16 through December 23, was assigned to each of the most pious monks. In the 1800s, a musical setting that would accommodate the stanzas and the refrain "Rejoice! Rejoice! Emmanuel shall come to thee O Israel" was fashioned out of some plainsong sequences. (There was no refrain in the original Latin.) And, since plainsong has no measures and no specified rhythmic scheme, the quality of this hymn is always flowing and free.

O Holy Night *Page 172*
(Words by John Sullivan Dwight; Music by Adolphe Charles Adam)

It is difficult to realize now that when "O Holy Night" was written by Adolphe Charles Adam, the 19th-century French composer who is best known for his ballet Giselle, *it was frowned on by church authorities. One French bishop even went so far as to denounce it for its "lack of musical taste and total absence of the spirit of religion." Despite this, it has become the most popular of all Christmas solos. Adam's friend and collaborator, the poet Cappeau de Roquemaure, was the first to supply a text for the melody, titling it "Cantique de Noël." The English words we use today, which made the tune "O Holy Night," were written by an American clergyman and musical authority named John Sullivan Dwight.*

Once in Royal David's City *Page 185*
(Words by Mrs. C. F. Alexander; Music by H. J. Gauntlett)

Cecil Frances Alexander took her position as an Anglican bishop's wife very seriously. She accompanied her husband throughout Ireland, scolding the wicked and praising the good, and most of all working with the youngsters, for whom she wrote a number of little poems and hymns. Her most famous collection was published in 1848 – Hymns for Little Children *– and it was here that "Once in Royal David's City" first appeared. A year later, H. J. Gauntlett discovered Mrs. Alexander's poem and set it to music. The city, of course, is Bethlehem, the birthplace of Jesus and of His ancestor King David.*

What Child Is This? *Page 182*
(Words by William Chatterton Dix; Music Traditional)

"Greensleeves," the tune to which "What Child Is This?" is sung, has a long history. It was apparently first licensed or registered in 1580 to a Richard Jones (with a set of lyrics that were not in the least religious, nor even very respectable), but it is probably older still. Some theories have it that Henry VIII wrote the song. In any event, Henry's daughter Queen Elizabeth I is said to have danced to it; Shakespeare mentioned it by name twice in The Merry Wives of Windsor; traitors were hanged as hired bands of musicians played its strains in lugubrious tempo. Almost three centuries later, about 1865, William Chatterton Dix published "The Manger Throne." Three stanzas were later culled from that poem and fitted to "Greensleeves," thus creating "What Child Is This?," one of our loveliest carols.

While Shepherds Watched Their Flocks by Night *Page 188*
(Words by Nahum Tate and Nicholas Brody; Music by George Frederick Handel)

George Frederick Handel's oratorio Messiah, *first performed in 1742 in Dublin, made the composer's name a symbol for the finest in religious music. A century later, Handel's fame was still at its height, particularly in the United States, where admirers such as the composer Lowell Mason were willing to attribute their works to him in order to secure a wider audience. Another composer, Richard Storrs Willis (famous for "It Came Upon the Midnight Clear"), who was attracted by the stately vigor of an aria from* Cyrus, *one of Handel's 46 operas, adapted as text a scriptural paraphrase by Nahum Tate and Nicholas Brody published in 1696. The result was "While Shepherds Watched Their Flocks by Night," which hews so closely to the Christmas story as told in the Bible that it was one of only six hymns allowed by the starchy church authorities of that day to be sung by congregations (in addition, of course, to the regulation canticles).*

I Saw Three Ships

Traditional

Note: For added interest, this arrangement can be played as follows:
*1st time: Play top line of right hand only. (**p**)*
*2nd time: Play both lines of the right hand, again without the bass. (**mf**)*
*3rd time: Play complete arrangement including piano bass and organ pedals. (**f**)*

1. **p** I saw three ships come sail - ing in On
2. **mf** And what was in those ships all three On
3. **f** The Vir - gin Mar - y and Christ were there On

(1) Christ - mas Day, on Christ - mas Day. I saw three ships come
(2) Christ - mas Day, on Christ - mas Day? And what was in those
(3) Christ - mas Day, on Christ - mas Day; The Vir - gin Mar - y and

(1) sail - ing in On Christ - mas Day in the morn - ing.
(2) ships all three On Christ - mas Day in the morn - ing?
(3) Christ were there On Christ - mas Day in the morn - ing.

O Holy Night

Words by John Sullivan Dwight
Music by Adolphe Charles Adam

Slowly and solemnly

1. O ho-ly night, the stars are bright-ly shin-ing; It is the night of the dear Sav-ior's birth. Long lay the world in sin and er-ror pin-ing, Till He ap-peared and the soul felt its worth. A thrill of hope, the wea-ry soul re-joic-es, For

2. Led by the light of faith se-rene-ly beam-ing, With glow-ing hearts by His cra-dle we stand. So led by light of a star sweet-ly gleam-ing, Here came the wise men from the Or-ient land. The King of Kings lay in low-ly man-ger, In

3. Tru-ly He taught us to love one an-oth-er; His law is love and His gos-pel is peace. Chains shall He break, for the slave is our broth-er, And in His name all op-pres-sion shall cease. Sweet hymns of joy in grate-ful chor-us rise we, Let

p smoothly

ped. sim. throughout

mp

Angels from the Realms of Glory

Words by James Montgomery; Music by Henry Smart

1. An - gels from the realms of glo - ry Wing your flight o'er
2. Shep - herds in the fields a - bid - ing, Watch - ing o'er your
3. Sag - es, leave your con - tem - pla - tions; Bright - er vis - ions
4. Saints be - fore the al - tar bend - ing, Watch - ing long in

(1) all the earth. Ye who sang cre - a - tion's sto - ry
(2) flocks by night. God with man is now re - sid - ing;
(3) beam a - far. Seek the great de - sire of na - tions;
(4) hope and fear. Sud - den - ly the Lord de - scend - ing

(1) Now pro - claim Mes - si - ah's birth.
(2) Yon - der shines the___ in - fant Light.
(3) Ye have seen His___ na - tal star.
(4) In His tem - ple___ shall ap - pear.

Come and wor - ship,

come and wor - ship; Wor - ship Christ the new - born King.

Guitarists: Play chords finger style.

174

Lo, How a Rose E'er Blooming

Traditional; Arranged by Dan Fox

Guitarists: Play chords finger style.
**Smaller hands may substitute cue note for bass note.*

JOSEPH DEAREST, JOSEPH MILD

Traditional

1. Jo - seph dear - est, Jo - seph mild, Help me rock my
2. Glad - ly dear - est, Mar - y mine, I will rock your
3. Lull - a, lull - a, lull - a - by, *(Hum)*

After last verse only

Christians, Awake, Salute the Happy Morn

Words by John Byrom; Music by John Wainwright

Guitarists: Play chords finger style.

The Holly and the Ivy

Traditional

Gaily

1. The hol-ly and the i-vy, When they are both full-grown, Of
2. The hol-ly bears a blos-som As white as lil-y flow'r, And
3. The hol-ly bears a ber-ry As red as an-y blood, And

(1) all the trees that are in the wood, The hol-ly bears the crown.
(2) Mar-y bore sweet Je-sus Christ To be our sweet Sav-ior. The
(3) Mar-y bore sweet Je-sus Christ To do poor sin-ners good.

ris-ing of the sun And the run-ning of the deer, The

play-ing of the mer-ry or-gan, Sweet sing-ing in the choir.

As Lately We Watched

Traditional

With spirit

1. As late-ly we watched o'er our fields through the night, A
2. His throne is a man-ger, His court is a loft, But
3. Then shep-herds be joy-ful, sa-lute your new King; Let

(1) star there was seen of such glo-ri-ous light.
(2) troops of bright an-gels in lays sweet and soft,
(3) hills and dales ring to the song that ye sing.

(1) All through the night an-gels did sing, In
(2) Him they pro-claim, our Christ by name, And
(3) Blessed be the hour, wel-come the morn, For

(1) car-ols so sweet of the birth of a King.
(2) earth, sky and air straight are filled with His fame.
(3) Christ our dear Sav-ior on earth now is born.

What Child Is This?

Words by William Chatterton Dix
Music Traditional

Very gently, but not dragging

1. What
(2. Why)
(3. So)

(1) Child is this,___ who laid to rest,___ On
(2) lies He in___ such mean es - tate___ Where
(3) bring Him in - cense, gold and myrrh;___ Come,

(1) Mar - y's lap___ is sleep - ing? Whom an - gels greet___ with
(2) ox and ass___ are feed - ing? Good Chris - tian, fear___ for
(3) peas - ant king,___ to own___ Him. The King of Kings___ sal -

GOOD CHRISTIAN MEN, REJOICE

Words by John Mason Neale; Music Traditional

Once In Royal David's City

Words by Mrs. C. F. Alexander; Music by H. J. Gauntlett

O COME, O COME EMMANUEL

Traditional

Quietly, with great feeling

in flowing style

1. O come, O come Em - man - u - el And
(2. O) come, Thou Rod of Jes - se, free Thine
(3. O) come, O Day - spring come and cheer Our

(1) ran - som cap - tive Is - ra - el That mourns in lone - ly
(2) own from Sa - tan's tyr - an - ny. From depths of Hell Thy
(3) spir - its by Thine ad - vent here, And drive a - way the

While Shepherds Watched

Words by Nahum Tate and Nicholas Brody
Music by George Frederick Handel

Their Flocks by Night

As with Gladness Men of Old

Words by William Chatterton Dix; Music by Conrad Kocher

Section Seven
Christmas Round the World

All Hail to Thee *Page 206*
(Words by Ernest W. Olson; Music by Philipp Nicolai)

Philipp Nicolai, a 16th-century Lutheran minister, was a pastor and eloquent preacher at such centers as Westphalia and Hamburg in Germany. There he wrote a number of hymns and tunes, including what have been called the King and Queen of the Chorales, "Wachet Auf" (Sleepers, Awake) and "Wie schoen leuchtet der Morgenstern" (How Bright Appears the Morning Star). Both of these hymns were used by Johann Sebastian Bach for church cantatas. Three centuries after Nicolai wrote the melody used here, Ernest Olson, a Swedish-born Lutheran who was taken to Illinois by his parents as a boy, wrote several stanzas for the melody and made of it one of our most inspiring Christmas hymns, "All Hail to Thee."

Bring a Torch, Jeannette, Isabella *(Traditional)* *Page 192*

The music for "Bring a Torch, Jeannette, Isabella" — a French carol with an ancient tune — has been known since the 14th century, not originally as sacred music, but as a ritournelle, or lively court dance in ¾ time. The words, too, are traditional, still sung today in France, chiefly in Anjou and Burgundy. The carol, with words and music, first appeared in a fascinating compilation of Christmas music, Cantiques de Première Advenement de Jésus-Christ, published in 1553 by a wealthy French count whose hobby was the collection of Christmas music. The charming text of this carol perhaps inspired the famous Georges de La Tour painting of the Nativity, in which two serving-maids look on from a distant corner of the stable.

Buon Natale (Merry Christmas to You) *Page 208*
(Words and Music by Bob Saffer and Frank Linale)

The sounds and aromas of Christmastime in Italy are exactly the same as ours — the bells ringing in the church steeple, the people from the hills greeting their neighbors from the valley, and the preparation of a feast for Christmas Day (only the feast, with its wine and pasta, is different from ours). And the essential ingredient, in St. Peter's Square or Peoria, on this molto bella holiday, is people, people wishing each other — in whatever language — "Merry Christmas." Nat King Cole made a best-selling recording of this effervescent song that Bob Saffer and Frank Linale wrote in 1959. The two strains of this lilting melody are reminiscent of several old favorites that have achieved folk-song status — "La Spagnola," a popular Italian dance tune, and "The Bowery," an American favorite of the gaslight era.

Burgundian Carol *Page 204*
(French Carol; English lyrics and Music adaptation by Oscar Brand)

Canadian-born songwriter and folksinger Oscar Brand first heard this carol from Maria Leach, editor of The Encyclopedia of Folklore, *who suggested that it would make an interesting American song. The original words and music were written by Bernard de La Monnoye, a French scholar and poet best known for his collection of Burgundian carols, published in 1701. Brand translated and reconstructed the lyrics and then altered the old French melody to fit his own easygoing folk-style of singing. He sang the "Burgundian Carol" one day on his radio show when his guest was Pete Seeger of The Weavers. Seeger loved the song and included it in The Weavers' best-selling Christmas record album. It was recorded later by Joan Baez, the Mormon Tabernacle Choir and Brand himself.*

The Coventry Carol *(Traditional)* *Page 196*

The music of "The Coventry Carol" dates from the 16th century and was taken from a pageant put on by shear-men and tailors of Coventry, England, on the steps of the city's cathedral between 1534 and 1584; this in turn was based on a much older morality play that tradesmen mounted for the entertainment of their monarchs and town officials. The song's minor tune and gently lulling words were sung in the play by the women of Bethlehem shortly before King Herod's men came to slaughter their infant sons in an attempt to kill the newborn "King of the Jews." In many churches, those children who were killed by Herod are commemorated today on December 28, the feast day of the Holy Innocents.

The Friendly Beasts *(Traditional)*

This lovely, simple song with its charming narration is a favorite of children at Christmastime. It dates from 12th-century England and is set to a tune that probably originated in medieval France. In it, the animals that were present in the stable in Bethlehem where Jesus was born – the donkey on which Mary rode, the cow that gave up its manger, the sheep that provided wool for a blanket, the dove that cooed the Baby to sleep, the camel that brought the Wise Men from the East – sing of the gifts they gave to the Infant King.

Hey, Ho, Nobody Home *(Traditional)*

"Hey, Ho, Nobody Home" probably dates back to the 16th century, though its origins are obscure. We do know that it is from England and was a favorite of carolers who went from door to door at Christmastime, soliciting food and drink in exchange for their harmony. This version can be sung and played as is, or in the form of a three-part round. Each of the three parts is cued on the music with a number in a square to indicate when each voice should enter.

Mele Kalikimaka (The Hawaiian Christmas Song)
(Words and Music by R. Alex Anderson)

This song about a different kind of Christmas, one that will be "green and bright," comes to us from Hawaii. It is the work of R. Alex Anderson, a successful Hawaiian businessman who wrote songs as a hobby. Although his best-known song is "The Cockeyed Mayor of Kaunakakai," his other tunes usually focus on the soft beauty of the Islands– "Lovely Hula Hands," "White Ginger Blossoms," "Lei of Stars." Bing Crosby and The Andrews Sisters made a recording of this swinging bit of Christmas sentiment.

O Come, Little Children
(Words and Music by Christoph von Schmidt and J. A. P. Schulz)

Christmas is, above all, a children's holiday, and many hymns are addressed to children, reminding them that the real reason for the sugarplums and Christmas trees is the celebration of the birth of the Christ Child. Christoph von Schmidt, who wrote the words to this carol, was known in his native Germany for the books on morals and religion that he wrote for children. The melody was written by Johann Abraham Peter Schulz, himself a child prodigy who at 15 went to Berlin to study under Johann Philipp Kirnberger, an organist who had been a student of Johann Sebastian Bach.

O Sanctissima *(Traditional)*

"O Sanctissima" is part Christmas carol and part church motet, set to a melody called "The Sicilian Mariner's Hymn to the Virgin," which may be Italian, English, or even Sicilian. No one knows, sometimes, where tunes originate, or when words become attached to a particular melody. This lovely tune is such a mystery. "O Sanctissima," with its original Latin text, was first published in 1794 in the United States. Today, the opening bars are familiarly known for their use in the song "We Shall Overcome."

Pat-A-Pan *(Traditional)*

Man-of-letters Bernard de La Monnoye is chiefly remembered for his collection of Burgundian carols, written in the local dialects that at one time flourished in central France. One of the carols in that collection is "Pat-A-Pan," a little homily to two boys who learn about praise and about the unity of God and man by playing their flute and drum together. Like a bagpipe drone, the drum's "pat-a-pan" sounds throughout the music, while above it the perky melodic line, a very ancient one, dances like the sound of flutes. "Pat-A-Pan" was first published in English in 1907. A modern Christmas song in much the same pattern and dealing with another musical lad is Harry Simeone's "The Little Drummer Boy" (see page 156).

'Twas in the Moon of Wintertime (The Huron Christmas Carol)
(English words by J. E. Middleton; Original Huron words by Father Jean de Brébeuf; Music Traditional)

" 'Twas in the Moon of Wintertime," generally considered the first Canadian carol, was originally written in the Huron Indian language in 1640 and set to an old French tune by a Jesuit priest, Jean de Brébeuf. In retelling the story of the Nativity, Father Brébeuf used symbols and figures that could be understood by the Hurons, and the hymn entered the tribe's oral tradition. It was sung by the Hurons in Ontario until 1649, when the Iroquois killed Father Brébeuf, wiped out the Jesuit mission and drove the Hurons from their home. In Quebec, to which many of the Hurons escaped, the carol re-emerged and was translated into English and French. This version is still sung today throughout Canada and is considered such a national treasure that it has been celebrated on a set of Canadian postage stamps.

Bring a Torch, Jeannette, Isabella

Traditional

Brightly

pp cresc.

G **Am** **G** **D7** **G**

mf

Bring a torch,— Jean-nette, Is-a-bel—la; Bring a
Has-ten now,— good folk of the vil—lage; Has-ten

D7 **G**

torch,— come swift-ly and run. Christ is born, tell the
now,— the Christ-Child to see. You will find Him a-

folk of the vil - lage; Je - sus is sleep - ing in His
sleep in the man - ger; Qui - et - ly come and whis - per

cra - dle. Ah, ah, beau - ti - ful is the
soft - ly, Hush, hush, peace - ful - ly now He

Moth - er; Ah, ah, beau - ti - ful is her
slum - bers; Hush, hush, peace - ful - ly now He

1. Son._____

2. sleeps.

193

(The Hawaiian Christmas Song)

Mele Kalikimaka

Words and Music by R. Alex Anderson

Brightly

Me-le Ka-li-ki-ma-ka is the thing to say___ On a bright Ha-

wai-ian Christ-mas Day._____ That's the is-land greet-ing that we

send to you___ From the land where palm trees sway.___

Here we know that Christ-mas will be green and bright,

The sun to shine by day and all the stars at night.

Me-le Ka-li-ki-ma-ka is Ha-wai-i's way To say "Mer-ry

Christ-mas to you."___ you."

The Coventry Carol

Traditional

Gently, like a lullaby

O Sanctissima

Traditional

Guitarists: Play chords finger style.

197

O Come, Little Children

Words and Music by
Christoph von Schmidt and J. A. P. Schulz

Moderately slow

p 1. O come, lit-tle chil-dren, from cot and from hall; O come to the
mp 2. The hay is His pil-low, the man-ger His bed; The beasts stand in
mf 3. Now "Glo-ry to God" sing the an-gels on high, "And peace up-on

(1) man-ger in Beth-le-hem's stall. There meek-ly He li-eth the
(2) won-der to gaze on His head. Yet there where He li-eth, so
(3) earth" heav'n-ly voic-es re-ply. Then come, lit-tle chil-dren, and

(1) heav-en-ly Child, So poor and so hum-ble, so sweet and so mild.
(2) weak and so poor, Come shep-herds and wise men to kneel at His door.
(3) join in the lay That glad-dened the world on that first Christ-mas Day.

Guitarists: Play chords finger style.

The Friendly Beasts

Traditional

Tenderly

1. Je - sus our broth - er, kind___ and good, Was hum - bly
2. "I," said the don - key, shag - gy and brown, "I car - ried His
3. "I," said the cow, all white___ and red, "I gave Him my

(1) born in a sta - ble rude, And the friend - ly beasts___ a -
(2) moth - er up hill and down; I___ car - ried her safe - ly to
(3) man - ger for___ a bed; I___ gave Him my hay___ to

(1) round___ Him stood, Je - sus our broth - er, kind___ and good.
(2) Beth - le - hem town." "I," said the don - key, shag - gy and brown.
(3) pil - low His head." "I," said the cow, all white___ and red.

4. "I," said the sheep with curly horn,
"I gave Him my wool for His blanket warm;
He wore my coat on Christmas morn."
"I," said the sheep with curly horn.

5. "I," said the dove from the rafters high,
"Cooed Him to sleep that He should not cry;
We cooed Him to sleep, my mate and I."
"I," said the dove from the rafters high.

6. "I," said the camel, yellow and black,
"Over the desert, upon my back,
I brought Him a gift in the Wise Men's pack."
"I," said the camel, yellow and black.

7. Thus every beast by some good spell,
In the stable dark was glad to tell
Of the gift he gave Emmanuel,
The gift he gave Emmanuel.

199

hey, ho, nobody home

Traditional–Fox

Moderately, with spirit

1. Hey, ho, no-bod-y home;
mp gradually getting louder

2. Meat nor drink nor
   Hey, ho,

mon-ey have I none,
no-bod-y home;

Yet will I be
Meat nor drink nor
3. Hey, ho,

mer — ry.____
mon-ey have I none, etc.(*)
no-bod-y home; etc.(**)

| Gm | Dm7 | Gm | Dm7 | Gm | Dm7 |

Hey, ho, no-bod-y home;
f

Meat nor drink nor

(*)*Continue as first voice from measure 5.*
(**)*Continue as first voice from measure 3.*

mon-ey have I none, Yet will I be mer — ry.

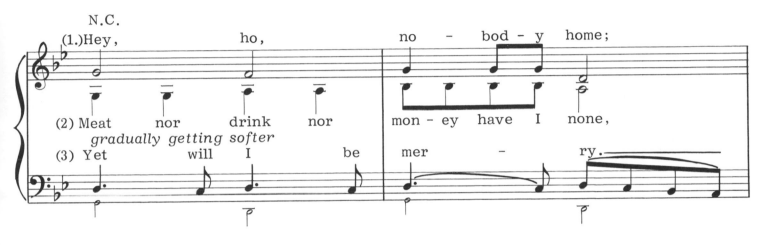

N.C.

(1.) Hey, ho, no - bod - y home;
mon-ey have I none,

(2) Meat nor drink nor
gradually getting softer
(3) Yet will I be mer — ry.

(1.) Meat nor drink nor mon-ey have I none, Yet will I be

(2) Yet will I be mer — ry.
(3) (hum)
(hum)

(1) mer — ry. (hum)

ppp

8va

sfz
Hey!
(*All shout*)

'TWAS IN THE MOON OF WINTERTIME

(The Huron Christmas Carol)

English words by J. E. Middleton
Original Huron words by Father Jean de Brébeuf; Music Traditional

1. 'Twas in the moon of win-ter-time when all the birds had fled, That (1) might-y Git-chi Man-i-tou sent an-gel choirs in-stead. Be

2. With-in a lodge of bro-ken bark the ten-der Babe was found. A (2) rag-ged robe of rab-bit skin en-wrapped His beau-ty round. And

3. O chil-dren of the for-est free, O sons of Man-i-tou, The (3) Ho-ly Child of earth and heav'n is born to-day for you. Come

(1) fore their light the stars grew dim, and won-d'ring hunt-ers heard the hymn:—
(2) as the hunt-er braves drew nigh, the an-gel song rang loud and high:—
(3) kneel be-fore the ra-diant Boy who brings you beau-ty, peace and joy:—

Chorus

Je - sus, your King, is born; Je - sus is

born! In ex-cel-sis glo-ri-a!

D.S. %

Stanza 1 in Huron

Estennialon de tsonoue
Jesous ahatonhia
Onnaouateoua d'oki
N'onouandaskouaentak
Ennonchien skouatrihotat
N'onouandilonrachatha
Jesous ahatonhia.

Burgundian Carol

French Carol; English lyrics and Music adaptation by Oscar Brand

(1) How man - y ox - en and don - keys now, If they were there when
(2) How man - y ox - en and don - keys now, ___ Dressed in er - mine,
(3) If we, like ox - en and don - keys then, In spite of all the
rushing ahead *more leisurely*

(1) first___ He came, How man - y ox - en and don - keys you
(2) silk___ and such, How man - y ox - en and don - keys you
(3) things___ we've heard, Would be like ox - en and don - keys
rushing ahead

(1) know, At such a time would do the same?___ 2. And
(2) know, At such a time would do as much?___ 3. As
(3) then, We'd hear the truth, be - lieve His word. ___
more leisurely

Last time only

All Hail to Thee

Words by Ernest W. Olson
Music by Philipp Nicolai

All hail to thee O bless-ed morn, To tid-ings long by proph-ets borne. Hast thou ful-fill-ment giv — en, O sac-red and im-mor-tal day, When un-to earth in glo-rious

(He) comes for our re-demp-tion sent, And by His glo-ry heav'n is rent To close up-on us nev — er; Our bless-ed Shep-herd He would be, Whom we may fol-low faith-ful-

(Merry Christmas to You)
BUON NATALE

Words and Music by
Bob Saffer and Frank Linale

Moderately, with spirit

Guitarists: Play chords finger style.

PAT-A-PAN

Traditional

Briskly

Am E7 Am E7 Am

1. Wil – lie, take your lit – tle drum; Rob – in, take your flute and
2. When the men of old – en days Gave the King of Kings their
3. God and man this day be – come Joined as one with flute and

mp – mf

E/A E E/A E Am

(1) come. When we hear the tune you play Tu – re – lu – re –
(2) praise, They had pipes on which to play Tu – re – lu – re –
(3) drum. Let the hap – py tune play on Tu – re – lu – re –

Em E E/A E

(1) lu, pat – a – pat – a – pan; When we hear the tune you
(2) lu, pat – a – pat – a – pan. They had drums on which to
(3) lu, pat – a – pat – a – pan. Flute and drum to – geth – er

Am G C E7 Am

(1) play, How can an – y – one be glum?
(2) play, Full of joy on Christ – mas Day.
(3) play As we sing on Christ – mas Day.

Section Eight
Christmas Folk Songs and Spirituals

Children, Go Where I Send Thee (*Traditional*)

Jean Ritchie, best-known member of the Ritchie Family of Kentucky, who have been singing authentic folk songs for generations, made this charming carol known to the world. It had been discovered in Kentucky in a country school for black children, where it may have been sung for the past three centuries. The verses, which sound like a child's counting game, actually tell the children of God how to go about preaching the gospel. Another version of this same carol also exists, thought to have been brought to the United States by Cornishmen who worked in the copper mines along Lake Superior.

Go Tell It on the Mountain (*Traditional*)

To black slaves in the United States, the birth of a Savior who would set all men free was a miracle to be sung about. And when there was something so notable to tell, what better place to tell it from than a mountain, just as Jesus had chosen for His Sermon on the Mount. "Go Tell It on the Mountain," an authentic spiritual that dates probably from the early 1800s, was first popularized in 1879 by the Fisk University Jubilee Singers. This chorus traveled throughout the United States and Europe at the end of the last century, earning scholarship-fund money for Fisk, a school founded to educate freed slaves.

I Wonder As I Wander (*Words and Music by John Jacob Niles*)

John Jacob Niles, the singer and collector of folk songs, said that he based his "I Wonder As I Wander" on a line or two of haunting music that he heard sung by a young girl in a small North Carolina town. He asked her to sing the few notes over and over, paying her a few pennies each time, until he had jotted it all down in his notebook. So close was the finished song to its Appalachian inspiration that Niles is often cited as arranger of the tune rather than its creator. The melody's minor key, minor intervals and unfinished cadences, as well as the poem's questioning pensiveness, make this one of the most plaintive of carols.

Rise Up, Shepherd, and Follow (*Traditional*)

"Rise Up, Shepherd, and Follow" might be called an American shepherd carol. It closely resembles a European shepherd carol, with the principal singer giving out the line and the chorus repeating the refrain. This spiritual was popularized in the United States by the distinguished American soprano Dorothy Maynor, who recorded with Serge Koussevitsky and The Boston Symphony, made national and international tours, and founded the Harlem School of Music in New York City. She also helped familiarize Americans with several other Negro spirituals about the birth of Jesus.

Sweet Little Jesus Boy (*Words and Music by Robert MacGimsey*)

Robert MacGimsey's tender lullaby looks at Jesus' birth and sees the Babe as He would become in adulthood, a man of sorrows. The world, not knowing who He was, would reject Him; that's the way it treats others; that's the way it is "down here." MacGimsey, who wrote such other songs as "Shadrack," a 1938 hit for Louis Armstrong, wrote "Sweet Little Jesus Boy" on Christmas Eve, 1932, after a dispiriting walk past crowded speakeasies in New York City. MacGimsey intended his lullaby as an art song, but it has instead joined the company of quasi-spiritual songs.

Go Tell It on the Mountain

Traditional

1. When I was a sin-ner, I prayed both night and day; I
2. When I was a seek-er, I sought both night and day; I
3. Down in a low-ly man-ger The hum-ble Christ was born; And

(1) asked the Lord to aid me, And He showed me the way:
(2) asked the Lord to help me, And He taught me how to pray.
(3) God sent out sal-va-tion That bless-ed Christ-mas morn.

Go tell it on the moun-tain, O-ver the hills and ev-'ry-where;

Go tell it on the moun-tain, Our Je-sus Christ is born.

I WONDER AS I WANDER

Words and Music by John Jacob Niles

Very simply and expressively

mp

1. I

Am   **F**   **Cmaj7**   **Am7**   **D**   **(E)**

(1) won - der   as   I   wan - der   out   un - der   the   sky   How
(2) Mar - y   birth-ed   Je - sus, 'twas   in   a   cow's   stall,   With
(3) Je - sus   had   want - ed   for   an - y   wee   thing,   A
(4) won - der   as   I   wan - der   out   un - der   the   sky   How

Am   **Am-6**   **Am6**   **Am-6**

(1) Je - sus   the   Sav - ior   did   come   for   to   die.   For
(2) wise   men   and   farm - ers   and   shep - herds   and   all.   But
(3) star   in   the   sky   or   a   bird   on   the   wing,   Or
(4) Je - sus   the   Sav - ior   did   come   for   to   die.   For

214

Children, Go Where I Send Thee

Traditional

Continue similarly

6. Six for the six that couldn't be fixed,

7. Seven for the seven that went up to heaven,

8. Eight for the eight that stood at the gate,

9. Nine for the nine that got left behind,

10. Ten for the Ten Commandments,

Rise Up, Shepherd, and Follow

Traditional

Moderately and rather freely throughout

There's a star in the East on Christ-mas morn; Rise up, shep-herd, and

(If you) take good heed to the an-gel's words, Rise up, shep-herd, and

fol-low. It will lead to the place where the Sav-ior's born;

fol-low. You'll for-get your flocks; you'll for-get your herds;

Sweet Little Jesus Boy

Words and Music by Robert MacGimsey

Slowly

Sweet__ lit-tle Je-sus Boy, They made You be born in a man - guh.
(man - ger)

p simply, like a lullaby

Sweet__ lit-tle Ho-ly Chil',__ Did-n't know who You wus.
(was)

Did-n't know You'd come to save us Lawd, To take our sins a - way. Our

eyes wus bline; We could-n't see; We did-n't know who You wus.
(was blind) (was)

*Guitarists: Tune 6th string down to D.

220

Section Nine
Christmas Classics and Instrumental Favorites

Brazilian Sleigh Bells *(Music by Percy Faith)* Page 245

The idea of sleigh bells in Brazil is, of course, absurd. But as a musical joke, it makes very good sense indeed – particularly when the person telling it is writer-arranger-conductor Percy Faith. The Toronto-born Faith, who was active in films, radio, television and recordings from the 1940s until his death in 1976, also found time to pen a number of songs, including a share of hits. His combination of jingling bells and Brazilian rhythms is a rare and unexpected treat for Christmastime.

Break Forth, O Beauteous, Heavenly Light Page 243
(Words and Music by Johann Rist and Johann Schop; Harmonized by Johann Sebastian Bach)

One of Martin Luther's principal resolves when he set out to reform the Church in the late 15th century was to involve people more deeply in the celebration of the Mass. To this end, he developed the Lutheran chorale, a religious hymn sung in four-part harmony by the congregation as part of the service. Johann Sebastian Bach made great use of the idea; at intervals in his pieces, he would insert a chorale for the congregation to sing – sometimes one he had written, sometimes one from the hymnal. "Break Forth, O Beauteous, Heavenly Light" is one of the latter. It was written by Johann Rist and Johann Schop in the mid-17th century, so that by 1734, when Bach included it in his Christmas Oratorio, *it was well known to congregations. The harmonization, however, is Bach's own.*

March of the Kings *(Traditional; arranged by Noble Cain)* Page 233

The Crusades – those religious expeditions to rescue the holy places in Palestine from the Moslems – created an enormous interest in both faith and fighting in the Middle Ages. French peasants from Provence in the 13th century, when the tune for this "March of the Kings" was being sung and danced to, must have endowed the Three Kings of the Christmas story with all the virtues and appearance of their own folk heroes nearer at hand. These were the French dukes, clad in gleaming armor, carrying brilliant banners and bejeweled shields, who fought for the Pope far more willingly than they would have for the lives of their own serfs. Hence the martial references in this text, sung to a tune that is perhaps even older than the verses. Georges Bizet, composer of the opera Carmen, *used the same tune as a farandole, or stately dance, in his incidental music for Alphonse Daudet's play* L'Arlésienne (The Woman from Arles).

March of the Toys *(Music by Victor Herbert)* Page 224

The surprising success of a musical based on L. Frank Baum's The Wonderful Wizard of Oz *prompted Irish-born composer Victor Herbert in 1903 to write* Babes in Toyland, *his musical comedy about two children, Jane and Alan, who escape from a miserly uncle to the garden of Contrary Mary and thence to the enchantments of Toyland. The plot was flimsy, but it suited the public taste of the moment, and the other characters – drawn from such sources as Mother Goose and others – were all applauded rapturously. Besides the lullaby-like "Toyland" and "I Can't Do the Sum," Herbert's score included the whimsically stiff-legged and strutting instrumental "March of the Toys."*

Nutcracker Sweets (Waltz of the Flowers/Arabian Dance/Trepak) Page 235
(Music by Peter Ilyich Tchaikovsky; adapted and arranged by Dan Fox)

Christmas would not be Christmas without The Nutcracker, *Peter Ilyich Tchaikovsky's beloved ballet for children. For this, the third of his great ballets, he chose one of the tales of E.T.A. Hoffmann, a story with a Christmas setting, about a young girl who dreams of her favorite gift from the holiday tree, a nutcracker. In Clara's reverie on Christmas Eve, the nutcracker becomes a handsome prince who whisks her off to a mythical Kingdom of Sweets, where she not only can gorge herself on sticky candies and elaborate cakes to her heart's content but can also be entertained by an endless succession of dancers and acrobats. In the spring of 1892, the Russian Musical Society reminded Tchaikovsky of his promise to compose a new work for one of its concerts. The composer had no time to begin from scratch; so he grouped a miniature overture and several dances from his new ballet into a suite and conducted it for the first time on March 19. The concert was a stunning success. Thus,* The Nutcracker Suite *became known even before the first production of the entire ballet, which was presented at the Maryinsky Theater in St. Petersburg at Christmastime in 1892. For this book, arranger Dan Fox has chosen three of the six "sweets" in the suite: the lavish, whirling "Waltz of the Flowers," a tribute by the flower attendants of the Sugar Plum Fairy; the sinuous Arabian dance called "Coffee"; and the Trepak, a wild and zestful Cossack dance.*

Section Nine: Christmas Classics and Instrumental Favorites

Parade of the Wooden Soldiers   *Page 227*
(Words by Ballard Macdonald; Music by Leon Jessel)

Leon Jessel caught the jaunty strut of toys exactly when he wrote his "Parade of the Wooden Soldiers" as a novelty item in 1905. It was published in Germany and apparently heard there by a Russian producer who was readying a new revue for Paris bearing the title La Chauve-Souris (The Bat), *for which he needed an offbeat dance number. He chose Jessel's rakish "Parade." The Bat opened on Broadway, finally, in 1922, and Ballard Macdonald, who wrote songs for the George White Scandals of 1924 and Ziegfeld's Midnight Frolic, gave the tune lyrics that although seldom heard anymore are included here. The arm-swinging melody and strutting rhythm of the piece make the march a charming one for children and adults at Christmas or any time of the year.*

The Skaters Waltz (Les Patineurs) *(Music by Émile Waldteufel)*   *Page 230*

Émile Waldteufel, the Waltz King of France, composed more than 250 waltzes, arranging the more popular ones for piano solo, so that the bourgeoisie could dance in their parlors while the nobility whirled away in the royal ballrooms. One of his most frequently heard waltzes is "Les Patineurs" (The Skaters). Waldteufel wrote it in 1882, at a time when Parisian society had developed a passion for ice skating, and the tune has remained to this day a waltz that can be heard wherever music is played for skating (ice or roller).

The Virgin's Slumber Song   *Page 240*
(English words by Edward Teschemacher; Music by Max Reger)

Some songs written especially for Christmas become so well known that they eventually are thought of as folk songs. "The Virgin's Slumber Song" is an example of just the opposite turn of events. Originally a folk-song melody to the words "Joseph Dearest, Joseph Mild" (see page 170), this graceful air was taken by the German composer Max Reger and transformed in 1912 into an art song, "The Virgin's Slumber Song," or "Maria Wiegenlied." Edward Teschemacher supplied an English translation of this lovely song, which echoes part of "Joseph Dearest, Joseph Mild": the Virgin Mary singing to her Baby while He sleeps. The rhythm of both melody and accompaniment suggests the rocking of a cradle.

March of the Toys

Music by Victor Herbert

Moderate march tempo

Parade of the Wooden Soldiers

Words by Ballard Macdonald
Music by Leon Jessel

Parade of the Wooden Soldiers

(The Parade)

THE SKATERS WALTZ

(Les Patineurs)

Music by
Émile Waldteufel

The Skaters Waltz

March of the Kings

Traditional; Arranged by Noble Cain

Nutcracker Sweets

(Waltz of the Flowers/Arabian Dance/Trepak)

Music by Peter Ilyich Tchaikovsky
Adapted and arranged by Dan Fox

Waltz of the Flowers

Moderately

Arabian Dance

Allegretto

The Virgin's Slumber Song

English words by Edward Teschemacher; Music by Max Reger

Gently, in one (each bar = 1 slow beat)

pp

A - mid the ros - es

Mar - y sits and rocks her Je - sus-Child,

While a-

ped. simile throughout

mid the tree - tops sighs the breeze so warm and mild,

And soft and sweet - ly

Guitarists: Play chords finger style.

The Virgin's Slumber Song

Break Forth, O Beauteous, Heavenly Light

Words and Music by Johann Rist and Johann Schop
Harmonized by Johann Sebastian Bach

Brazilian Sleigh Bells

Music by Percy Faith

Bright samba ($\quad$ =1 beat)

Brazilian Sleigh Bells

(p) gradually getting louder

Section Ten
Ring Out the Old! Ring In the New Year!

The Scottish "Auld Lang Syne" can be translated as "old long ago" – which is also a lovely way of putting it. For most people, New Year's Eve just isn't complete without the singing of "Auld Lang Syne." Thanks to Guy Lombardo and His Royal Canadians, who first played it on their New Year's Eve radio broadcast in 1929, the song is New Year's Eve, with the special memories it evokes for each individual. The words were adapted in the late 18th century by Scottish poet Robert Burns from traditional Scottish songs, but the composer of the melody is unknown. For decades, people have agreed that it makes a bonny way to close the "old long ago" of Christmastime and usher in the hopes and resolutions of a brand-new year.

"For Thy Mercy and Thy Grace" was written early in the career of Henry Downton, who enriched English hymnody with original verses and translations of French and Swiss hymns. Downton was the son of a minor official at Trinity College, Cambridge, and received his bachelor's degree there in 1840. The next year, he wrote "For Thy Mercy and Thy Grace," calling it "A Hymn for the Commencement of the Year." The tune, "Posen," to which Downton set his words, had been written more than 100 years earlier by Georg Christoph Strattner, a leader in the German Reformed Church.

Alfred, Lord Tennyson is considered the most representative poet of the Victorian Age in England, and many of his works characterize the conflict between the Christian faith and the beginnings of the scientific revolution. The death of his sister's fiancé, Arthur Henry Hallam, at the age of 22 plunged Tennyson into profound shock and a lifelong struggle between faith and doubt. "Ring Out, Wild Bells," generally considered a New Year's hymn, is taken from the 106th Canto of In Memoriam, Tennyson's monumental elegy to Hallam that was published in 1850, the same year that he was appointed Poet Laureate. The melody was once thought to have been based on Wolfgang Amadeus Mozart's Twelfth Mass. However, modern scholars agree Mozart did not compose the work and attribute it variously to the relatively obscure Carl Zulehner or Wenzel Müller.

Christmas has come, Christmas has just about gone, Christmas has been full of friends and carols and food and gifts, but now it's time to wonder "What Are You Doing New Year's Eve." Frank Loesser, whose Broadway hits included Where's Charley?, Guys and Dolls, The Most Happy Fella and the 1962 Pulitzer Prize-winning musical How to Succeed in Business Without Really Trying, wrote "What Are You Doing" in 1947. It was introduced that year in a recording by Margaret Whiting.

What Are You Doing New Year's Eve

Words and Music by Frank Loesser

RING OUT, WILD BELLS

Words by Alfred, Lord Tennyson; Music Traditional

For Thy Mercy and Thy Grace

Words by Henry Downton; Music by Georg Christoph Strattner

Firmly, without dragging

AULD LANG SYNE

Words by Robert Burns; Music Traditional

Index of First Lines

Also Available
❋ from Reader's Digest ❋

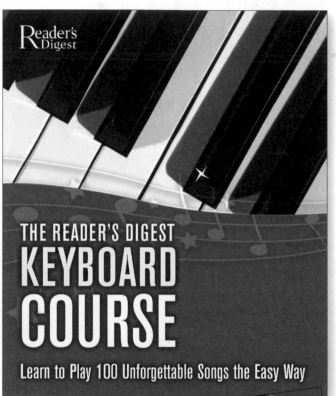

The Reader's Digest Keyboard Course

Designed especially for the person who reads little or no music, this color-coded songbook—containing 100 songs—will make playing the piano or keyboard as easy as 1, 2, 3. Each song contains blue notations for beginners and black notations for more experienced musicians—with stickers to place on the keys to help beginners find the right note every time.

ISBN(13) 978-0-7621-0688-2 • $30.00

Lift Every Voice and Sing

Here are 150 inspirational songs that invoke faith, patriotism, nature, and friendship. Spiral bound to lie flat, this collection includes unique arrangements with vocal and easy-to-play piano lines, plus melody lines for guitar, violin, flute, oboe, or harmonica accompaniment, plus a 32-page lyric book.

ISBN(13) 978-0-7621-0618-9 • $30.00

Children's Songbook

Great for all ages, this book is a delightful collection of familiar songs that children love to sing. This 252-page illustrated songbook is spiral bound to lie flat and has easy-to-read sheet music for more than 130 songs, along with fascinating facts about each one, plus a 40-page lyric book and a 12-track CD. Includes musical games and activity ideas to add to the fun.

ISBN(13) 978-0-7621-0619-6 • $30.00

Reader's Digest Books are distributed by Penguin Group (USA) Inc. and can be purchased through retail and online bookstores nationally.

For more information or to order books, call: 1-800-847-5515.